The Land of Six Philosophies

SHABDAVERSE
VOLUME 5

Ashish Dalela

The Land of Six Philosophies —SHABDAVERSE Volume 5
by Ashish Dalela

Published by Shabda Press
press.shabda.co
ISBN 978-93-85384-54-7

SHABDA
PRESS

Contents

Series Preface

SHABDAVERSE is a series of article collections, organized by topics. The articles in these collections were originally published online on the SHABDA website over many years. A series of articles written from 2014 to 2019 were earlier published in chronological order under the series title *Western Questions Eastern Answers*. The SHABDAVERSE series organizes articles from 2019 to 2025 by categories, rather than dates. This is for multiple reasons—(a) there are enough articles in each category to produce collections organized by categories, (b) readers wanting to read topic-focused collections might find this approach more convenient and cohesive than the chronological one, and (c) the topic-focused approach allows us to make unique covers for each book, after all, in the ultimate analysis, a book is judged by its cover!

All these articles follow an interdisciplinary approach to every topic—everyday experience, empirical evidence, problems with different ideas advanced in the past and present, how ideas may have evolved historically, how certain issues were seen and understood differently across cultures, and with a solution to any and all related open and unsolved problems, which can be validated through ordinary experience, empirical evidence, and rational arguments. I often cite statements and ideas from Vedic texts, not to substantiate my claims, but to establish that my ideas are not new, and that I as the author of these articles don't claim authorship of the ideas. I only aim to present ancient ideas in a modern language, so that present audiences may understand and appreciate them based on what they already trust.

Pursuant to the science-religion divide created during European Enlightenment, we see two opposite approaches to the study of ancient texts—(a) the religious approach takes an ancient text as a divine revelation to be trusted on faith at best, and (b) the scientific approach, which rejects these texts as the personal opinion of dogmatic scribes, unprovable through or contradictory to the available evidence, and focuses on collecting evidence, followed by speculation to find an explanation that fits that evidence.

The Vedic tradition differs from both of these. Ancient texts have been preserved in a written form for thousands of years, but in every successive era, those texts were explained through commentaries. The texts and the commentaries were never merged. That trend continues today, and those who like to read ancient texts with explanations can do so. However, these explanations do not contrast their ideas with those in present-day sciences and religions, because the Vedic tradition was historically inward-looking, not outward-looking. By continuing the same trend, commentaries on Vedic texts appear to most people as different ideas, not better or true ideas, when contrasted to the ideas found in other worldviews. In fact, those ingrained in other worldviews consider Vedic texts primitive because the Vedic ideas don't match the ideas they have received through their culture and education. Therefore, the inward-looking historical trend of the Vedic texts is not adequate for the present time. For the present time, the Vedic tradition must become outward-looking, and contrast itself to the ideas of the other worldviews.

Therefore, in these articles, we—(a) sometimes we begin with unsolved problems created by prevalent ideas and theories and try to solve them using reasoning and evidence, and then connect the solution to the ideas in ancient texts, and (b) sometimes we begin with ideas and theories in ancient texts and show how they are relevant to the present time by showing how they solve unsolved or open problems.

I have seen with consternation a tendency among many authors to take ancient ideas, reformulate them in convenient ways, disconnect them from the sources from where these ideas were taken, and present these ideas as an author's original work. I think that this approach constitutes a theft, disrespectful to the teachers and texts from where ideas were taken. But more importantly, it filters the tradition of texts and teachers through the opinionated lens of the author who takes ideas without attribution, and closes the door for readers to go back to the tradition for more exploration in the future. Authors with such attitudes present themselves as prophets of original ideas, while masking the actual prophets.

I aim to show people of the present time a path to the Vedic tradition, not pretend to be a prophet of original ideas. Personally, I'm convinced that everything I have written about is a miniscule fraction of all that can be written, understood, or derived from the Vedic texts, and hopefully, future generations will do more of what I have tried to do. My primary goal is to dispel the myth that the Vedic texts are like the texts of other religions which have to be accepted on faith, rather than reason and observation. I call the dispelling of this myth, the *scientific study of Vedic texts*, pursuant to the common definition of science as truth based on reasoning and evidence, in contrast to a religion based on blind faith or belief.

Ashish Dalela

Nature is Pregnant with Possibility – The Doctrine of Satkāryavāda

The following are excerpts from Sāñkhya Sūtras on the doctrine of Satkāryavāda. This is important for anyone interested in Sāñkhya. The full text is available as Material and Spiritual Natures.

Topic 40
सत्कार्यवाद नरिूपणं
satkāryavāda nirūpaṇaṃ
The Description of Satkāryavāda

Sutra 1.111
वादविप्रितपित्तेःतदसद्धिरितिचेत्
vādivipratipatteḥ tadasiddhiriti cet

vādi—the wise; eva—in this way; pratipatteḥ—describe; tat—of that (prakriti); siddhiriti—the doctrine; cet—know.

TRANSLATION

The wise describe the doctrine of that (prakriti) in this way; know that.

PURPORT

The term 'sat' means eternal, and 'kārya' means effect. So, the doctrine of Satkāryavāda states that the effect eternally exists within the cause (prakriti) and is manifest from it. Thus, everything that is visible in nature originally existed within the cause (prakriti). Alternately, nothing new is ever created, although it is manifest or unmanifest. For example, if we see a new building that wasn't previously visible, it is not something that did not previously exist. Rather, it exists eternally as a *possibility* within prakriti, and is manifest from it. The observed changes are thus the conversion of a possibility into reality.Sutra 1.112

तथाप्येकतरदृष्ट्या एकतरसिद्धेःनापलापः
tathāpyekataradṛṣṭyā ekatarasiddheḥ nāpalāpaḥ

tathā—thus; api—also; ekataradṛṣṭyā—one-sided vision; ekatarasiddheḥ—one-sided attainment; na—not; apalāpaḥ—denial or rejection.

TRANSLATION

Thus, with one-sided vision also one-sided attainment; this is not a denial or rejection (of the other side).

PURPORT

The doctrine of Satkāryavāda holds that the effect is immanent in the cause and emerges from it. This means that the cause is *sufficient* to produce the effect. This is a one-sided view of causality because to determine a cause, we must have both sufficiency and *necessity*. To say that X is a sufficient cause of Y, we can say that Y exists within X. But that doesn't mean that Y doesn't also exist in some other Z, which could also be a cause of Y. Thus, Satkāryavāda establishes the sufficiency of the cause, but not the necessity of the cause. To get necessity, we must have the reverse directional causality—i.e., from the effect to the cause, to say that no other cause could be the cause of this effect. That would establish the necessity in addition to sufficiency. The claim here is that we are only trying to establish the one-sided condition of causal sufficiency.

We can illustrate this problem by an example. Suppose that a child is born from a mother's womb. The condition of *sufficiency* would say that the mother is fully capable or sufficient to produce the child. But it is not necessary that the child be born from a specific mother. We could speculate: "Maybe the birth of this child from this specific mother is an accident. Maybe the same child could have been born from another mother". This speculation entails the idea that there are other potential causes that could have equally well produced the effect. For instance, we could say that the world could alternatively be produced by something other than prakriti. This sutra states that we are not trying to refute the idea that there could be alternative causes of the world—i.e., that prakriti is necessary for the world. We are just trying to establish *sufficiency*.

Sutra 1.113
त्रविधिवरीधापत्तेश्च
trividhavirodhāpatteśca

trividha—three-fold; virodhāpatteśca—also the counterarguments.

TRANSLATION

Also, there are three-fold counterarguments (against Satkāryavāda).

PURPORT

These counterarguments are discussed and refuted in the next topic. While a three-fold counterargument is noted here, actually five such viewpoints are noted in the next topic. The first two of these arguments fall into a ridiculous category, which is completely false. The next three arguments are plausible but not accepted by Satkāryavāda. The three-fold positions against Satkāryavāda refer to the last three positions. The ridiculous arguments are that something comes out of nothing automagically, or that something comes out of nothing based upon some rules (e.g., the laws of modern science). The plausible arguments are— (1) matter is an energy that can take any form, (2) a desire converts energy into a form, and (3) the combination of the capable (person) and the capacity (matter) creates an effect. They are all contrary to the Satkāryavāda doctrine in which the effect eternally preexists in the cause and is manifest from it. The prakriti in Sāñkhya philosophy is the feminine energy of the Lord. She is fully capable of producing everything, but She produces it based on God's will. The prakriti is not inert, or unconscious; She rather has a subordinate will.

Thus, something doesn't come out of nothing, because it preexists in prakriti. There is no rule which is constantly being applied to produce something new because things are working by Sakti's will. Likewise, everything is not possible always; rather matter grows through many stages of manifestation. A desire converts energy into a form, but it is not merely desire; there is an objective capacity that exists eternally in prakriti. Finally, there is a combination of a capable person (God) and the capacity (God's Sakti), but that combination is the Sakti doing something based upon God's will. It is not a sexual union without which the creation would be impossible (e.g., a man or woman alone cannot create a child, and a sexual union is needed; but such is not the case for prakriti since the prakriti is fully capable of creating, but She creates by God's will). We arrive at this nuanced view by considering all that is against Satkāryavāda.

Topic 41
असत्कार्यवादनिराकरणं
asatkāryavādanirākaraṇaṃ
The Abrogation of Asatkāryavāda

Sutra 1.114
नासदुत्पादो नृशृङ्गवत्
nāsadutpādo nṛśṛṅgavat

na—not; sat—that which is eternal; utpādo—being produced; nṛśṛṅgavat—just like a man's horn (i.e., that which is ridiculously impossible).

TRANSLATION

That which is not eternal (i.e., temporary) being produced just as a man's horn (i.e., that which is ridiculously impossible comes into existence).

PURPORT

The creation of that which did not previously exist is here compared to a man's horn. Generally, animals have horns, but men do not. So, this sutra sarcastically criticizes this doctrine of something being created without a previous existence or possibility as a man suddenly growing a horn. When animals that can have a horn are born, the horn doesn't exist. The horn subsequently grows in the animal. At birth, the horn exists in a state of potentiality but manifests subsequently. This potentiality doesn't exist in the men, so they don't grow horns. Thus, the doctrine of something being created out of nothing is rejected; if something is visible, there must be a preexisting potentiality that may be invisible, but it exists eternally as a potential, which is subsequently manifest.

Sutra 1.115

उपादाननियमात्

upādānaniyamāt

upādāna—that which is produced; niyamāt—due to a rule.

TRANSLATION

That which is produced (from the cause) due to a rule.

PURPORT

Here is the example of a classical physical scientific causality is taken. In Newton's theory of motion, for example, the next state of a particle is determined by the previous state, based on some rule—Newton's gravitational law. The next state doesn't preexist in the cause, but the rule produces the next state. The logical question is: Who computes the rule? In scientific theories, for example, there must be a computer or calculator which computes the effects of these rules on a continuous basis. A rule cannot be automatically implemented; even if we define the rule universally, it must still be continuously computed. But we don't know of a universal computer that computes all such rules. So, how are these rules causing the emergence of the effects from the causes?

Sutra 1.116

सर्वत्र सर्वदा सर्वासम्भवात्

sarvatra sarvadā sarvāsambhavāt

sarvatra—everywhere; sarvadā—always; sarvāsambhavāt—everything is possible.

TRANSLATION

Everywhere, always, everything is possible.

PURPORT

When the rule-based causal explanation fails in science because the effect doesn't seem to follow rules—e.g., the same cause can produce many effects, and the same effect can be produced by many causes—then, one might resort to the idea that everything is always possible everywhere. Modern scientists, for example, postulate that some reality randomly emerges out of a 'quantum vacuum'. The 'quantum vacuum' is therefore just some energy, but the *form* taken by this energy is not fixed. The same energy can potentially take any form, and hence anything can be created from an energy vacuum anywhere, anytime, because those effects are simply the alternative forms of the latent energy.

Similarly, the theory of evolution in biology postulates that things come out of nature due to random mutations. According to evolutionary theory, a new species of life does not preexist as a possibility (as the doctrine of Satkāryavāda would say). Rather, without a rule, some new things are created due to random mutations, because every type of mutation is always possible, everywhere. Why the mutation occurs cannot be explained, which is why it is called 'random'.

Satkāryavāda would counterargue that everything is not possible everywhere and all the time. Rather, certain things are possible, but when they become possible, they are easily and naturally manifest. For example, instead of saying that new species are created by random mutations, Satkāryavāda would state that the possibility for the species emerging becomes prominent in prakriti. When that possibility is not prominent, we cannot create it. Thus, for example, at the moment, dinosaurs cannot be created, even though they are possible. If all things were always possible, then dinosaurs could be created now. So, why did nature produce giant lizards in the past, and not presently?

Sutra 1.117

शक्तस्य शक्यकरणात्

śaktasya śakyakaraṇāt

śaktasya—the result of the capable or the powerful user; śakya—possibly; karaṇāt—the instrument.

TRANSLATION

Possibly the result of the capable use of the instrument (i.e., matter, by the powerful user).

PURPORT

Then there are those who attribute the manifestation of new things to some magical power that is so capable that it can produce anything from anything. This view is demarcated from the previous views, namely, something coming out of nothing, something happening due to a rule or law, and everything being possible everywhere. A good example of this doctrine is the *ex-nihilo* creation in Christianity in which God creates the world due to His infinite power. A similar type of doctrine is the Design Argument approach to explain the creation in which God's power is used to design the universe. Along with the arguments about something coming out of nothing, something happening due to a rule or law, and everything being possible everywhere, this argument is also bundled with those that are against the Satkāryavāda view.

We can say that in Satkāryavāda the possibility preexists in nature itself. Therefore, a beautiful flower is not the result of the design of a designer. It is rather a property of matter itself. However, that property exists in prakriti eternally and is sometimes manifest. Thus, all inventions, theorems, scientific theories, technologies, etc. are preexisting in prakriti eternally. We are not the 'creators' or 'inventors' of these things; we are simply 'discovering' them.

Sutra 1.118

कारणभावाच्च

kāraṇabhāvācca

kāraṇabhāvācca—also the desire being the cause.

TRANSLATION

Also, the desire being the cause.

PURPORT

Finally, the fifth idea that is contrary to Satkāryavāda is noted here as the ability of our desire to produce something new. This is similar to everything is possible everywhere, with one limitation, namely that the effect is not produced due to *randomness* (as in the previous case), but due to our *desire*. This idea is employed in John von Neumann's interpretation of quantum theory in which a 'choice' selects a possibility from the infinite sea of possibilities. The distinction is that the choice lies in the observer, and the possibility is matter. Thus, a soul-matter separation is necessary for this doctrine to be true.

We can illustrate the contrast to Satkāryavāda as follows. Suppose we say that that a knife is just a material instrument, and it can be used to either cut vegetables, or tighten a screw, or hurt somebody. All these differences in effects are simply the byproducts of our desire, and they don't exist *a priori* in the knife itself. The Satkāryavāda doctrine would instead say that the knife internally holds all these possibilities eternally, and they are occasionally manifest. So, in the former case, the desire *creates* an effect from the knife, and in the latter case, the desire *manifests* a preexisting possibility from the knife. The Sāñkhya claim is that the possibility of being used to cut vegetables, to tighten a screw, to hurt somebody, and infinite other use cases, are *objectively* present in the knife. Our desire only 'selects' one of these possibilities, and doesn't 'create' them.

But, at this juncture, the question arises: if our desire is manifesting something from prakriti, then our body must stop working when we go to sleep, because obviously at that time we are not making any choices. So, how can prakriti keep digesting food, the body can keep breathing, etc. even when we don't make a choice? And the answer to that problem is that prakriti is itself capable of producing the possibility because there is an innate choice within prakriti. So, the prakriti is not inert material 'stuff'. She is rather a conscious person.

Thus, without rejecting the matter-soul distinction, we must now say that there is a desire by which things are happening, but that desire in the soul is being fulfilled by the desire in the prakriti to allow the soul to enjoy the material world. Likewise, nature produces the world based on Her desire but directed by God's desire. Hence, the power of God's will need not be rejected, but that will power is not the only cause. Finally, everywhere, always, everything is possible is not rejected, but it is also subject to the will in God and His Sakti.

THE NYĀYA CONCEPTION OF A SCIENTIFIC THEORY

Below is the translation and commentary on some of the Nyāya Sutras, which describe the nature of a scientific theory as comprised of four aspects. The first aspect represents the purpose of the system; the second, the functional parts that execute this purpose; the third, a mechanism of control that translates the purpose into functional activities; and fourth, a system that maintains coherence in the system and allows it to persist over time. These descriptions can be easily understood if we think of 'science' as the description of a *system*–e.g., a human body, an organization, or a society–which embodies a purpose, has functional parts, a system of control to translate the purpose into action, and something that keeps the system cohesive over long periods of time. The general doctrine of such systems defines a "scientific theory" in Nyāya and it is radically different from mechanistic conceptions of scientific theories. The understanding of such non-mechanistic conceptions of science is important to those interested in alternative forms of scientific theories.

Sutra 1.1.26

तन्त्राधिकरणाभ्युपगमसंस्थितिःसिद्धान्तः

tantrādhikaraṇābhyupagamasaṃsthitiḥ siddhāntaḥ

tantra—a mechanism; adhikaraṇa—supervises; abhyupagama—the agreement; saṃsthitiḥ—a system or arrangement; siddhāntaḥ—a scientific theory.

TRANSLATION

A scientific theory is a mechanism that supervises or controls the agreement in a system or arrangement.

COMMENTARY

Modern science formulates theories of individual things, but Nyāya describes a theory or doctrine to be the explanation of a system or arrangement of things. This is a rejection of reductionism or the idea that the whole can be reduced to independent parts. Our bodies, for example, are complex arrangements in which each part performs a distinct function. By these functions, a coherent system is produced. But what keeps this system together? Why doesn't it break apart into pieces—like it should if the parts were independent? This is the fundamental role of propounding a doctrine. The world around us exists as coherent systems. These include the small cells in our body, their organization into organs, which then organize into our body. These bodies are collected into societies, which then exist as part of ecosystems, which collectively form a planet. What holds all these things together, and why do they exist cohesively? The explanation of this coherence and cohesion and the supervising mechanism that keeps things coherent and cohesive requires an explanation. The essential purpose of a scientific doctrine is to provide such an explanation. Innate in this description of 'science' is the idea that there aren't many theories of nature; there is rather one 'science' that explains how order emerges in nature. This order spans across many types of parts and their organization into a whole. This type of theory is called a General Systems Theory at present, which studies the world as organized systems rather than a collection of independent parts.

Sutra 1.1.27

सःचतुर्विधिःसर्वतन्त्रप्रतितिन्त्राधिकिरणाभ्युपगमसंस्थित्यिर्थान्तर भावात्

saḥ caturvidhaḥ sarvatantrapratitantrādhikaraṇābhyupagama-saṃsthityarthāntarabhāvāt

saḥ—that doctrine; caturvidhaḥ—four kinds; sarva—everything or the whole; tantra—mechanism; pratitantra—each mechanism; adhikaraṇa—the controlling system; abhyupagama—the agreeing; saṃsthiti—a system or arrangement; arthāntara—the difference of meaning; bhāvāt—exists.

TRANSLATION

That doctrine has four parts—the doctrine of the whole, the doctrine of each thing, the doctrine of a control system, and the doctrine of how things exist in agreement as a system or arrangement despite differences in meanings.

COMMENTARY

After describing the purpose of a scientific theory, this sutra further elaborates on the four aspects of such a theory. These four aspects are the whole, the parts, how the whole controls the parts, and how the parts remain coherently organized within the whole. To illustrate this idea, we can think of an institution or organization. The organization comprises many roles, some of which are higher while others are lower. The higher role controls the lower roles, and through this control, the organization attains the goals that it has set for itself. Nevertheless, the members of the organization can be replaced one by one, preserving the organizational structure. Thus, we can discern four distinct parts in an organization. First, there is a leader of the organization, who embodies the purpose of the whole organization. Second, there are members of the organization. Third, there is a system of governance in the organization due to which the goals of the organization are translated into the organization's activities. And fourth, there is a system that maintains coherence within the organization. Each of these four aspects will be further elaborated in the subsequent sutras.

By analogy, a scientific theory of nature must also describe reality as the composition of four distinct aspects—(a) the leader or purpose of the organization, (b) the member parts of the organization, (c) the system of governance in the organization by which the leader controls the organization, and (d) the method by which the organization maintains coherence in the face of ongoing change.

We can think of the same problem in terms of our bodies. The body has many parts such as hands, legs, stomach, chest, etc. However, the head is the leading part that controls the other parts. This control of the body is affected through the nerves that connect the head to the various parts of the body. And there is a system of immunity and hormones that keep the body coherent.

Here a broad non-reductionistic sketch of a system of organization is presented. In this sketch, there are many parts, but these parts are organized hierarchically, and therefore, the system has a hierarchical structure. The head at the top of this hierarchy controls this system through the hierarchy. Therefore, the hierarchy serves the purposes of functional control and the coherence between the parts. One key aspect of this sutra is the separation between the *control* system and the *coherence* system. In our body, for example, the control system is conscious, whereas the coherence system is unconscious. By the control system, we can direct our senses to act in various ways. But in addition, there is an unconscious system of health and immunity that keeps the system functioning. The implication of this sutra is that this should be the general model by which everything must be described. And a scientific theory is therefore defined to be that doctrine which supplies such a rational description.

Sutra 1.1.28

सर्वतन्त्राविरुद्धःतन्त्रे अधिकृतःअर्थःसर्वतन्त्रसिद्धान्तः

sarvatantrāviruddhaḥ tantre adhikṛtaḥ arthaḥ sarvatantrasiddhāntaḥ

sarvatantra—the whole system; aviruddhaḥ—not opposed; tantre—the system; adhikṛtaḥ—that rules over; arthaḥ—the purpose; sarvatantrasiddhāntaḥ—the principle of the whole system.

TRANSLATION

The system that rules over the purpose of the whole system and is not opposed to the whole system, is the principle of the whole system.

COMMENTARY

Again, we can understand this sutra by the example of an organization's leader who controls the organization. The leader represents a part of the system, and yet the whole system, because he or she represents the purpose for which the system exists. Every organization is formed for a certain purpose. That purpose then expands into a structure of functional roles. And those functional roles are then populated by individuals. The leader embodies all three of these. First, his goal is the fulfillment of the organization's goals. Second, he is the head of the organizational structure. Third, he is a member of the organization.

Similarly, the head in the body holds the goal for the existence of the body. The head controls the rest of the body. And the head is a part of the body.

The only reason the head of an organization would be replaced is that his or her goals stopped being the goals of the organization, or he or she became incapable of administering the organization. Then the individual occupying the position of the organization's head would be replaced by another person. Therefore, the sutra states that the head must not be inconsistent with the rest of the system. Of course, in our bodies, we cannot easily replace the head. But in an organization, such replacements are fairly routine in modern times.

The system that represents the whole is not *physically* the whole in this case. The whole is rather semantically the *purpose* of the whole thing. This means that if we merely think of each of the parts, we might not see the purpose of its existence. But as we aggregate the parts, then the purpose becomes visible. The part of the whole that represents that purpose constitutes the 'whole'. In a physicalist doctrine, we would think of the whole as a physical aggregation of the parts. But in this sutra, this whole represents the purpose of the whole.

Sutra 1.1.29

समानतन्त्रसद्धिःपरतन्त्रासद्धिःप्रततिन्त्रसद्धिान्तः

samānatantrasiddhaḥ paratantrāsiddhaḥ pratitantrasiddhāntaḥ

samāna—the class or commonality; tantra—the system; siddhaḥ—the fulfillment; paratantra—the other system; asiddhaḥ—the non-fulfillment; pratitantra—every system; siddhāntaḥ—the principle.

TRANSLATION

The principle of every system (i.e., the parts) is that the fulfillment of the class or commonality of that system is the nonfulfillment of the (class or commonality) of the other systems.

COMMENTARY

We can understand this sutra by the example of the members of an organization. Each member of the organization (including the head of the organization) has a different role or function, which constitutes the 'class' of that member. For example, some person works in engineering, while others work in marketing, finance, human resources, manufacturing, etc. Even within the various departments of an organization, each person performs a unique role. Many such roles collectively fulfill the function or duties of the department. As a result, the members of an organization can be described in two ways. First, they are unique individuals or persons. Second, they have unique roles or organizational functions. Hence, we can call the head of the organization, the "CEO". Then we can have heads of sales, marketing, engineering, human resources, and so on. Similarly, we can designate each person in an organization by the role they play.

This sutra extends this idea to the study of all systems and defines the part of the system as something that always performs a unique role that is not performed by any other part in the system. Hence, that part can be designated by a different class in the system. By that designation, it also gets a unique name.

For example, a car comprises many parts such as the engine, transmission, gears, wheels, brakes, accelerator, steering, lights, seats, dashboard, etc. Each part is identified by a unique class, as they perform a unique function, not fulfilled by the other parts. Each part is also a materially individual thing. Thus, we can describe the world materially as these unique things. And we can describe the same world as unique functional roles. This sutra insists that the scientific theory must describe how the system or parts functions as a whole, which requires designating each part with a unique class of functionality.

Sutra 1.1.30

यत्सदि्धौ अन्यप्रकरणसदि्धिःसिःअधकिरणसदि्धान्तः

yatsiddhau anyaprakaraṇasiddhiḥ saḥ adhikaraṇasiddhāntaḥ

yatsiddhau—by the fulfillment of which; anyaprakaraṇa—the other events; siddhiḥ—fulfilled; saḥ—that; adhikaraṇasiddhāntaḥ—the principle of control.

TRANSLATION

By the fulfillment of which the other events are fulfilled, that is the principle of control.

COMMENTARY

A good example of a control system in the human body is the system of nerves and veins that transmit and receive control signals to and from the brain and the other parts of the body. The brain is the controller—just like the leader of an organization. The body parts such as hands and legs are the parts that are controlled by the brain—just like the members of an organization. And the veins and nerves are the control system whose sole purpose is to get something else to behave in a certain way. These veins and nerves form a parallel system to the one comprising of the parts, and they give the whole system a control structure. For example, in a car, when the brakes are pressed, a signal is transmitted to the wheels, which causes the wheels to stop. Likewise, when the accelerator is pressed, then a signal is transmitted to the engine, which increases the flow of gasoline into the engine. This system of signal transmission and reception, which is then used to control the parts is called the 'control' system.

Sutra 1.1.31

अपरीक्षिताभ्युपगमात्तद्विशेषपरीक्षणं अभ्युपगमसिद्धान्तः

aparīkṣitābhyupagamāttadviśeṣaparīkṣaṇaṃ abhyupagamasiddhāntaḥ

aparīkṣita—the untestable; abhyupagama—in coherence; attad—obtained or perceived; viśeṣa—the details or specifics; parīkṣaṇaṃ—the verification; abhyupagamasiddhāntaḥ—the principle of being coherent.

TRANSLATION

The principle of being coherent is the verification that the details or specifics (parts) are perceived to be in coherence by that which is not testable (i.e., that it remains invisible).

COMMENTARY

This sutra separates the principle of *control* from that of *coherence*. To understand this separation, we can think of a computer. The user interface of the computer—e.g., the buttons on an application—create signals which then control the rest of the computer. However, the computer also has an operating system that allows the control system, the intended purpose, and the various parts to function cohesively. The operating system, for instance, can forbid one part (that is not designated to control the whole system) from becoming the controller. The operating system gives fair access to all the parts to allow them to function. Its central role is to ensure that the computer doesn't crash, one part doesn't destroy the other parts, and parts are treated fairly in a system. The separation of the control and the coherence systems is like that between the purpose for which the system exists (e.g., the user interface which makes the system useful) and the fairness system which makes the system persistent (e.g., the operating system in a computer which manages the system's operations).

The system of coherence constitutes a set of rules that define the correct and incorrect operation of the system. In the case of a society, for example, these rules are meant to ensure that the society survives over time. The survival of the society is quite different from its other goals—such as prosperity, happiness, or other kinds of economic and political objectives. The government makes the decisions about the goals of the society. But another system must ensure that these pursuits do not destroy society. This is generally achieved by enacting a system of rules to be followed by every member of the society, including the government which controls the society, and the military, police, or bureaucracy, which translate the government's will onto the people as societal control. Hence, although the government is the controller of the society, it cannot act whimsically. Even though the police, government, and bureaucracy are controlled by the government, they cannot disobey the principle of society's existence.

A good analog of the coherence system would be the immune system in the body. Its central purpose is to ensure that the body has longevity. What we do with the body is not controlled by the immune system, and in that sense, there is a separation of the controlling system (e.g., the brain) and the coherence system (e.g., the system of hormones). The brain can for instance push the body to work very hard toward some goals, and the immune system will then trigger a collapse and force the body to rest for longevity.

Similarly, the principles of the health of society—namely, the moral principles of duty and responsibility—are independent of society's goals. If the goals force immorality on the society, then they jeopardize its longevity. In that sense, the laws of a society should not be whimsically changed because these laws are like the immune system that ensures that the body survives over time; the laws of the land should not be tailored to make it achieve different goals; these laws should be the principles of the health of the social system

The Nyāya Philosophy of Presence and Absence

The Nyāya system of philosophy describes a category called abhāva or 'absence' and then explains how bhāva or 'presence' manifests from the absence. This is a very long discussion in Nyāya Sutra (which I'm translating presently) and has many nuances. It is hard to capture all these details here, but I thought that instead of waiting for the book to be published, I can share an excerpt from that book. This doctrine of presence and absence is central to understanding how the Vedic system describes manifestation from the unmanifest. Basically, there exists a premise, which then gives rise to a question. Then the question gives rise to an answer, which then leads to another question, and so on. This excerpt discusses the relation between this process and the process of the transmigration of the soul, the production of new bodies, and God's creation of the world. All these varied ideas are based on the same essential insight, but it is very counterintuitive to modern thinking. How all these "religious" ideas become "scientific" ideas under the new way of thinking is quite useful and illustrative.

Sutra 4.1.14

अभावाद्भावोत्पत्तिर्नानुपमृद्य प्रादुर्भावात्

abhāvādbhāvotpattirnānupamṛdya prādurbhāvāt

abhāvāt—from the absence; bhava—the presence; utpattih—production; na—not; anupamṛdya—not to be destroyed; prādurbhāvāt—from the birth.

TRANSLATION

From the absence is the production of the presence. It is not true that (the old thing) is not to be destroyed from the birth (of the new thing).

COMMENTARY

The doctrine of 'absence' which we have discussed earlier, is revived again here, and as we have noted this 'absence' constitutes doubts, problems, questions, and incompleteness. The simple contention is that the problem arises first, and the solution is produced from the problem. The problem is like the seed, and the solution is manifest from within the problem. As is sometimes said, "necessity is the mother of invention", the necessity is the problem, question, doubt, and incompleteness. When we think of the material world as a substance, then every new substance must be the transformation of the old substance. The 'absence' of a substance cannot produce a new substance. That would constitute a classic "something from nothing" scenario. Therefore, these claims about absence-producing presence cannot be understood unless we change our thinking from substances to meanings. A question is a meaning and an answer is meaning. A question can give rise to an answer because the answer lies within the question, but the answer is hidden within the question.

This is a matter of practical realization that as our consciousness advances, we can see the answers to everything within the question itself. We just have to analyze, understand, and grasp the true nature of the question, and the answer becomes automatically visible in the question. This method of generating answers is often employed by people coaches. A trainee goes to a coach and asks him a question seeking guidance—e.g., about their career or life. But the coach doesn't provide an answer. He rather asks another question about the question which the trainee has asked, to clarify the trainee's question. This questioning by the coach forces the trainee to think about his or her question more deeply. As a result, some insight about the question is obtained, and the trainee gives an answer to the coach. Now, the coach asks another question about the previous answer, in light of the original question, in an attempt to further clarify the question. By this process of repeated questioning, rather than giving answers, ultimately, the trainee sees the answer on their own. This answer is not something that was given by the coach. The coach is not there to provide answers but to facilitate the thinking about the question because the belief is that the answer lies within the question. Hence, if the question is sufficiently clarified, then the answer would be automatically visible within that question itself.

This method is commonly applied to problems where the answers are quite personal. The belief is that if we provide an external answer, then the rebellious mind would reject the answer as something being imposed by others. Therefore, it is better that someone comes up with their own answers, facilitated by the questions of the coaches. This method is also used by Zen masters who instead of answering any question, only tell their disciple to think about paradoxes and puzzles, which then clarifies the nature of the question, and the answer is then seen within the question itself. The same method of generating answers becomes prominent when a person is situated in sattva-guna. Whenever a doubt arises, the person in tamo-guna asks someone else for a readymade answer, and the person in rajo-guna looks for an answer separate from the question—typically by analyzing various typical answers. The person in sattva-guna instead looks deeper into the question, and there he finds the answer.

So, the philosophy of 'absence' should not be viewed as gobbledygook. It rests on deep realizations about the nature of matter, predicated on the idea that matter is meaning, so it can generate new meaning. That generated thing lies within the generator in an unmanifest form. But if we look closer, we will find it. So, the process of generation is also the same—we have to look closer.

The problems of spiritual life are also like that. Instead of looking outward and seeking readymade answers, or trying out various things experimentally, we have to look deeper within. We are the problem, and we can be the solution. In fact, the solution lies within—if only we look deeper within. When we look outwardly, we get some readymade answers, but there is no conviction. Indeed, the arrogant mind asks people questions, only to counter-question and reject the answers. Thus, most people who call themselves "seekers" simply keep roaming from one place to another, trying to "learn" something new. But whatever is taught to them is taken superficially, and counter questioned. In this way, the search becomes infinite. A slightly more advanced person tests out various possible alternatives on their own and rules out many of them. He is more proactive, and by his proactiveness, he convinces himself about what the answer is *not*. Then, the person who is most serious goes deep into the question itself.

Once we grasp this idea in its various forms, then we can understand how the presence comes from the absence. It is not the creation of something from nothing, and the origin of everything is not nothingness. It is rather a question. As we have discussed, this question itself arises from some premise. It is a fact that a person who knows nothing cannot even ask good questions. Rather, the questions arise when something is known. Thus, there are regular teachers to impart the students' knowledge, so that they can ask intelligent questions. Then there are teachers who must push the students to find the answer within the question. And there can be teachers who can ask counter questions to challenge the supposed answers. Thus, all methodologies of knowing are available to us.

Buddhists and other voidists generally misrepresent the understanding of 'absence' as 'nothingness', because they too are thinking in terms of substances rather than meanings. If we accept the semantic way of thinking, then we can say that the material world springs from a question, a problem, an incompleteness, a doubt. It is an 'absence' which was in turn produced by a 'presence' and it is then capable of producing another presence. In this way, we must understand that there is absence inside presence, and presence inside absence.

As we have discussed before, God exists as the original premise, answer, solution, and completeness. But this existence is not *valuable* unless there is a question, problem, doubt, or incompleteness. Therefore, from the answer arises a question. When that question is turned back toward the premise, as we have discussed earlier, then it makes the original premise valuable, because now there is both demand (a question) and supply (an answer). If, however, the question is not turned back to the premise, then it leads to another question, another answer, and so on. Thus, when the soul turns towards God, he not only finds the answer but generates value. But if he turns away from God, then he neither finds answers nor does he generate any value. Rather, there is only a succession of questions and answers. In this way, everything manifests from God in the process of creating *value* but if the question and answer turn away from God, then that value is destroyed and an endless cycle of questions and answers are generated, which constitute material life. We cannot talk about value unless we talk about meaning. So, once we understand how everything is meaningful, then we can understand how some meaning is also valuable, and then we can grasp how that meaning was produced in the attempt to create value. This is the essence of saying that the presence emerges from the absence.

Once we understand how the question arises from an answer, and the answer arises from the question, then we can grasp the second part of this sutra, which says that the previous thing may be destroyed upon the manifestation of the new thing. In this case, when an answer arises from a question, the question can be destroyed. So, ultimately, what we see is a collection of answers, and we don't see the absence or the question, doubt, problem, or incompleteness. This is what leads to the 'substance' dogma which says that the world exists as things. But why did the world emerge? And the response is that it emerged from a question. But when the answer has appeared, then the previous question is destroyed. As time passes, therefore, all we get is a system of theories and doctrines, and we don't know the *reason* that they were originally created.

Therefore, a good way to learn a subject is to go into the history of the subject, understand both the problems and how they were addressed by the solution. If we don't understand the questions, then we get the *meaning* but we don't understand why it is *valuable*. Value exists in the relation between a problem and a solution, a question and an answer. But since the solution destroys the problem, therefore, we just get the meaning and not the value. As a result, the connection between the present reality and the past reality is seemingly gone. But it is not truly gone; the question is not truly destroyed if we see the *entire sequence* of questions and answers. The value in the answer depends on the question, and knowing the question clarifies the answer and vice versa.

This method of reasoning or logic constitutes the basic difference between Western and Vedic logical thinking. In Western logic, a premise leads to a conclusion, but in Nyāya philosophy, a premise creates a question, which then creates an answer, which then creates another question, and so on. Vedānta Sutra, for example, is called nyāya-prasthāna, because in every answer is hidden another question, and in every question is hidden an answer. How the unmanifest is revealed from within the manifest rests on this understanding of question and answer, meaning and value, hiding and revelation. This fundamental process of manifestation is here used to explain the succession of bodies. The implication is that every type of material body creates a problem. To solve that problem, another body is produced, and so on. So, the body change happens because none of the bodies are perfectly answering the problems of life. That problem appears in the subtle form as an 'absence' and then it manifests a gendered body and a gross body as the answer to that problem. So, this understanding of logic and reasoning is essential to understand all the doctrines in Vedic texts.

From this, we can also understand how the 'subtle' reality is like a question, and the 'gross' reality is like an answer to that question. To see the subtle reality, we have to ask deeper questions: Why do I exist? Why do I have this body? Why was I born in these situations? The reasoning and justification for the existence of the gross body are that there was an unanswered question that then led to this body. Therefore, when all the questions are answered satisfactorily then both the subtle and gross body will be destroyed. Since spiritual life is the only method that answers all the questions, it is the only way to stop the cycle of birth and death. Rebirth is thus ensured so long as the questions remain.

The Aspected Nature of the Absolute Truth

Below are some verses from the Nyāya Sutra that discuss the nature of the Supreme Lord, and describe how He is one and many, how He is attained by devotees and yet never truly attained by anyone, and how the varied aspects of His personality are hidden inside the other aspects, such that knowing any aspect is knowing the full truth in one sense, and yet not knowing it completely in another.

Sutra 5.1.2

साधर्म्यवैधर्म्याभ्यामुपसंहारे तद्धर्मविपर्ययोपपत्तेः साधर्म्यवैधर्म्यसमौ

sādharmyavaidharmyābhyāmupasaṃhāre taddharmavipa-ryayopapatteḥ sādharmyavaidharmyasamau

sādharmya—similar nature; vaidharmyābhyām—and opposing nature; upasaṃhāre—upon the destruction of; taddharma—that nature; viparyaya—its opposite; upapatteḥ–logically concluded; sādharmya—similar nature; vaidharmya—opposing nature; samau—being equivalent.

TRANSLATION

Upon the destruction of similar nature and opposing nature, that nature and its opposite are logically concluded; the similar nature and the opposite nature being equivalent.

COMMENTARY

Whether a mother scolds a child or feeds the child, the intention behind it is the same—she wants to protect and nurture the child. When a prudent teacher appreciates the student or reprimands him, the intention behind both these actions is the same—the teacher wants to produce a well-educated student. Whether a noble king gives prizes to people who have done good work or delivers punishment to those who have done bad work, his intentions are the same—to create a moral and principled society. In the same way, the Lord has to be understood as beyond the dualities of this material world. His rewards and punishments have the same purpose—to purify the soul; His care and neglect are meant to deliver the same result—to liberate the soul from material entanglements. And the knowledge He imparts to the devotees and the delusions of success and failure He creates for the materialists have the same purpose—to enlighten the humble and confuse those who are arrogant.

Those who are conditioned by material dualities are unable to see this nature of the Lord. So, they think: If the Lord is like this, then He cannot be like that. But they are baffled in their judgment because the Lord is both. Thus, this sutra states that when the mundane dualistic way of thinking is destroyed, then one realizes that the Lord has a nature and its very opposite; in fact, both natures are equivalent. So, the Lord is benevolent toward His devotees and harsh toward the demons; He teaches those who are inquisitive, and He deludes those who are arrogant; He is visible to those who are seeking Him, and He is invisible to those who want to avoid Him. The same person is all the potentialities and qualities, but all those potentialities and qualities are not simultaneously manifest. They are rather manifest in different relationships based on different attitudes. Since the Lord can manifest everything, therefore, He is everything—even opposing qualities. But since the Lord doesn't manifest everything simultaneously, therefore, He is not universally kind or harsh, visible or hidden, knowledge or delusion. Rather, He reveals Himself differently in various contexts. Thus, as the Absolute Truth, He is everything. But as some contextual revelation of this Absolute Truth, He is only one of the opposing qualities.

Thus, the Absolute Truth also becomes the contextual truth and if we combine all these contexts, then it seems that the Absolute Truth is self-contradictory. Therefore, we must recognize that the Absolute Truth is the *potentiality* for everything, but everything is not simultaneously manifest at the same time, place, situation, or in relation to every person. Thus, everyone can see the Lord differently, and yet, He is the one and the same person. This infinite nature of the Lord is understood by the person who has transcended the dualities of the material world. In this world, something is either hot or cold, either big or small, either heavy or light. But the Lord is all of these qualities simultaneously.

Sutra 5.1.3
गोत्वादगोसदिधवित्तत्सदिधः
gotvādgosiddhivattatsiddhiḥ

gotvāt—by being a cow; gosiddhivat—just like the attainment of a cow; tatsiddhiḥ–that (nature of the Lord) is also attained.

TRANSLATION

Just like the attainment of a cow by being a cow, that (nature of the Lord) is also attained.

COMMENTARY

The Absolute Truth follows the philosophy of tit-for-tat. If one is gentle and humble, then the Lord reveals His gentle and humble side. But if one is arrogant and proud of their power, then the Lord reveals a side that is also insensitive and very powerful. The cow is considered a very gentle animal in Indian culture. She gives milk, and therefore, she is like a mother. In the same way, if the soul becomes gentle and giving like the cow, the Lord also becomes caring and concerned toward the soul. This leads to a problem for many people. They ask: What is the Absolute Truth? And the answer is: He is whatever you are. You will see a nature of the Absolute Truth as a reflection of your nature.

Of course, every thief wants an honest accountant. Every killer wants to receive mercy. Every cheater wants to be given a fair trial. So, we may not like what we see. But that simply means that we have to change ourselves. We don't have to conjure some fancy, intricate, or complicated understanding of the nature of the Absolute Truth. We just have to *become* whatever truth we want to see. If something is hidden from our vision, then it is as good as not existing. So, if we never see the harsh side of the Lord, it is practically as if that nature doesn't exist. But, of course, it exists for those who are evil. So, the Absolute Truth is everything that we can imagine. And yet, He is one thing for each person. This means that there is great variability in the understanding of the Lord for each person. In one sense, there is nothing other than the Lord. If we receive harshness in our life, then that is a face of the Lord, which we are seeing due to our nature and past activities. And then if we see a successful and opulent life, that is also a face of the Lord that we are seeing due to our past actions.

Thus, the Lord is the only object; everything is some or the other face of the Lord. We are also a part of the Lord, therefore, when we see Him in a certain way, in one sense, He is seeing Himself. But of course, if the part has the choice to see a different face, then a different face of the Lord would be revealed to it. In this way, the Absolute Truth becomes self-conscious by desiring to see a different aspect of His personality, and then reveals that aspect to Himself.

Sutra 5.1.4

साध्यदृष्टान्तयोर्धर्मविकल्पादुभयसाध्यत्वाच्चोत्कर्षापकर्षवर्ण्
यावर्ण्यविकल्पसाध्यसमाः

sādhyadṛṣṭāntayordharmavikalpādubhayasādhyatvāccot-
karṣāpakarṣavarṇyāvarṇyavikalpasādhyasamāḥ

sādhya—the achieved; dṛṣṭāntayoh—the vision; dharma—nature; vikalpāt—from the alternative; ubhaya—both; sādhyatvāt—from the object to be known; ca—also; utkarṣa—elevated; apakarṣa—degraded; varṇya—classes; avarṇya—classless; vikalpa—the alternative; sādhya—the object to be known; samāḥ–equivalent.

TRANSLATION

From the object to be known, both the vision that is achieved, and the alternative to that nature can be attained. Also, elevated and degraded, the classes and the classless, are equivalent alternatives in the object to be known.

COMMENTARY

This sutra continues the description of the Absolute Truth. The meaning of 'absolute' is that it is the potentiality for all the relative truths, and it can reveal anything that we can imagine, think, desire, or choose. The Lord is the source of the elevated spiritual world and the degraded material world. He is the source of the classful society of this world, where some people are higher than others, and the lower class serves the higher class. And He is the source of a classless or egalitarian society of the transcendental world where everyone serves everyone else, and they take pleasure in pushing each other forward and upward. Thus, the unity is the source of the diversity, but that unity is *everything* rather than one thing or nothing. The impersonalist thinks that the Absolute Truth is one thing—Brahman—and it is devoid of all the qualities, including personal individuality. And the voidist says that the ultimate truth is nothing—i.e., devoid even of consciousness. But these philosophies are rejected by all Vedic texts. Yes, there is a unity, which is devoid of duality in the sense that the Absolute Truth is *everything*. But that truth reveals itself differently to different individuals based on their nature, preferences, desires, and choices.

Sutra 5.1.5

कचित्सिाधर्म्यादुपसंहारसदि्धेर्वैधर्म्यादप्रतषिेधः

kiṃcitsādharmyādupasaṃhārasiddhervaidharmyādapratiṣed-hah̤

kiṃcit—a little; sādharmyāt—from the similar nature; upasaṃhāra—destruction; siddheh—achieved; vaidharmyāt—from the opposing nature; apratiṣedhaḥ—is not forbidden.

TRANSLATION

It is not forbidden to say that from a little bit of similar nature, from (within the opposing nature), the destruction of the opposing nature is achieved.

COMMENTARY

There are two kinds of aspect theories of reality. In the first, the aspect of an object is different from the object. For example, we can think of a particle and its properties. Each property of the particle is an aspect of the particle, but even if all the properties are removed, the particle remains. This type of aspect theory constructs a hierarchy between the property and the particle. This hierarchical theory of aspects is used in Sāñkhya while describing the material world. For example, the tanmātra or properties like shape, size, and color are aspects of the sense of seeing; likewise, red, green, and blue are aspects of color. The senses are the aspects of the mind; etc. This hierarchy, as we have noted earlier, produces an inverted tree in which the trunks are aspects of the root, the branches are the aspects of the trunks, and so on. When we come to the root, however, there cannot be aspects; the root has to be that one thing without any aspects. This kind of aspect theory of reality doesn't work for the Absolute Truth when that truth is itself said to have aspects. Now, we have to look at the second aspect theory, in which one aspect is hidden inside the other aspect, and can manifest from within. When the hidden aspect manifests, then it absorbs the visible aspect within it, and that visible aspect now becomes the hidden aspect.

To understand this idea, we can think of multiple-personality disorder. Suppose that a person has two personalities—one good and the other evil. When the good side manifests, the evil side is hidden inside the good side. But when the evil side manifests, then the good side is hidden within the evil side. Now, if we apply the first type of aspect theory, then we would say that there is a "person" who is different from both good and evil sides, and that person chooses one of these sides and remains aware of which side has been chosen. But this doesn't happen in the case of multiple-personality disorder because the person who changes these personalities isn't merely putting on an act of being good and evil, being fully aware of the other side of their personality. They are rather completely unaware of the existence of the other personality aspect.

This second type of personality aspect theory is used in the yin-yang model where there are two opposite traits—yin and yang—and the yin exists as a small thing inside yang, while the yang exists as a small thing inside the yin. The 'smallness' can be seen as the depiction of something that lies unmanifest, and the 'bigness' can be viewed as the depicture of that which is currently manifest.

Thus, yang exists inside the yin but is unmanifest, and yin exists inside yang and is unmanifest. So, when yin transforms into yang, then the cause of the transformation is not 'outside' yin. It was rather the yang property that existed in an unmanifest form within the yin property. This unmanifest becomes manifest and it "swallows" what was previously manifest. The result of this aspect theory is that yin and yang are just properties, and there is no need for an "object" that holds them as its properties but is different from the properties.

Thus, in the first type of aspect theory, there is a hierarchy, which ends at the root, and that root cannot have many aspects. But if the root itself has to be aspects, then we need another kind of aspect theory in which one aspect lies hidden within the other aspect, and when it manifests, it swallows the other aspect. In this way, one person can have many personality types, such that when one personality type is revealed, the other types are hidden. These personality types are not the aspects of some deeper-level reality. They are rather the byproducts of hiding many aspects within an aspect, such that all the aspects are present within each aspect; however, they remain invisible.

This sutra describes such an aspect theory in relation to the Absolute Truth, which is the root of the inverted tree. All these aspects are not the properties of some deeper-level object. They are rather the full object. One nature exists in a minute form within the manifest nature, but it is unmanifest. Then, when it starts growing, it completely absorbs the previously visible nature, such that it becomes minute and hidden inside. Thus, this sutra states that even if something exists in a minute form, it can grow and make the thing that is big and visible totally invisible. However, that invisible thing now becomes the minute reality within the visible, and it too can manifest subsequently, thereby, reversing the manifest-unmanifest relation. Ironically, the minute seed that grows to swallow the manifest nature preexists hidden within the manifest nature.

This kind of idea has been depicted in many traditional philosophies as the snake that eats its own tail. The part that is eaten becomes hidden within the part that eats. What is generally not shown is that the tail also becomes the head, and the head becomes the tail, and the process can then also be inverted.

Sutra 5.1.6

साध्यातदिशाच्च दृष्टान्तोपपत्तेः

sādhyātideśācca dṛṣṭāntopapatteḥ

sādhya—the object to be known; atideśāt—from a place beyond; ca—also; dṛṣṭānta—the occasions of experience; upapatteḥ–are logically created.

TRANSLATION

Also, from the place beyond (the reach of anyone), the object to be known logically creates the occasions of experience.

COMMENTARY

This sutra talks about the first type of aspect theory that we referred to in the last sutra, which are the aspects in the sense that properties are aspects of an object. Thus, the term 'also' is used, which, in the context, means that both types of aspect theories are applicable. The second type of aspect theory refers to the nature of the Lord, and the first type of aspect theory refers to the experience of the Lord by other living entities. To understand these two descriptions, we have to delve into the forms of the Lord as described in the Vedic texts.

These forms are known as Narayana, Vasudeva, Saṅkarṣaṇa, Pradyumna, and Aniruddha. Similarly, the forms are also known as Narasimha, Kūrma, Vārāha, and Vāmana. All these forms are based on the aspect theory of the first type, in the sense that they are called the parts, the part of the parts, and the part of the parts of the whole truth—Krishna. Then, each of these forms displays many different moods. For example, when Narasimha appeared, He was in the most ferocious form, and a very angry mood. He continued in that angry mood, even after killing Hiranyakaśipu, until His devotee Prahalad offered Him prayers and pacified His anger. Then, the same Narasimha became just like a loving father, and He placed Prahalad on His lap just like a father would do for his son. He then affectionately proceeded to place His hands on Prahalad's head as if to assure him to not be afraid because he has the most powerful protector. These two aspects of the Lord—one fearsome and the other loving—are the aspects of the same person, but they are aspects in the second type of aspect theory. When one aspect manifests, then the other aspect becomes hidden.

But the aspects in the first type are simultaneously manifest. Thus, there are infinite Vaikuṇṭha planets in which the various forms of Lord Viṣṇu are present simultaneously. These are the first types of aspects. Then, in each aspect, there are many moods and personas which are manifest one after another. This manifestation requires us to understand the aspect in the second way. For example, in the Goloka planet, Krishna goes to the forest to graze His cows with His friends, and He becomes invisible to His mother and father for some time. Then in the evening He returns to His father's place and becomes visible to His father and mother again. So, the same person transforms by hiding and revealing His varied personality aspects. These are the second type of aspects. Thus, both types of aspect theories have to be understood to fully understand the Lord.

Some people accuse the Vedic religion of "polytheism" because they don't understand how reality is described to have many aspects. The variegated nature of the Lord's persona is alien to other religions, which think of God as the "father in heaven". Of course, God is the father too. But that is one of the aspects. He is also a son, friend, lover, mentor, teacher, master, and even a servant. For example, Krishna is a servant to His father, and He fetches His father's slippers because He doesn't want Him walking barefoot. That doesn't mean that God is a servant to everyone. But if we become His servant, then by becoming the cow, the cow nature of the Lord is revealed to us. Therefore, God has innumerable forms either due to these forms being the eternally manifest aspects in different planets or due to various moods of the form being manifest one after another. This is the science of the Absolute Truth and it is unique to the Vedas, and the science is simply that the Absolute Truth is everything, but everyone doesn't see the same thing. So, the Absolute Truth is *not* a Universal Truth—i.e., He is not the same for everyone. He is the collection of all the relative truths, which means that everyone can see Him in different ways, and those visions of the Lord are not fictitious or imaginary. They are all visions of the truth.

In Christianity, Islam, and other similar religions, the idea of God is married to the idea of a Universal Truth. "There is no God but our God". If you don't accept our God, then we shall kill you. The idea of Universal Truth comes from Greeks, and Romans married this idea to Christianity to create an impoverished vision of God as a Universal God. Then they proceeded to kill and enslave other people in the name of religion. This claim is also sometimes called Neoplatonism and it is used to explain the manifestation of the world from God, but ultimately it is a false idea because the aspects of God are not understood. The tolerant nature of the Vedic religion comes from an alternative doctrine of God, in which He reveals Himself to us according to our nature. So, there are potentially infinite visions of God, because the seekers are also infinitely varied. This alternative understanding of God is called "Absolute Truth" rather than "Universal Truth". Universalism is the basis on which ideologies are imposed on others. But all Vedic texts, including Nyaya philosophy, reject this idea.

Sutra 5.1.7

**प्राप्य साध्यमप्राप्य वा हेतोःप्राप्त्याविशिष्टत्वादप्राप्त्यासाधकत्
वाच्च प्राप्त्यप्राप्तिसमौ**

**prāpya sādhyamaprāpya vā hetoḥ prāptyāviśiṣṭatvādaprāpty-
āsādhakatvācca prāptyaprāptisamau**

prāpya—the thing to be achieved; sādhyam—on achieving; aprāpya—remains unachieved; vā—alternatively; hetoḥ–the purpose; prāptya—on attaining; aviśiṣṭatvāt—from the universal; aprāptya—not achieved; asādhakatvāt—as if being unachievable; ca—also; prāpti—achievement; aprāpti—non-achievement; samau—are equivalent.

TRANSLATION

On achieving the thing to be achieved, the thing remains unachieved. Alternatively, from attaining the purpose, the universal is not achieved, as if being unachievable. Also, achievement and non-achievement are equivalent.

COMMENTARY

The philosophical understanding of the Universal Truth is predicated on the belief that there is an "idea" which we can grasp by our minds, and by that grasping, we have "conquered" that truth by the powers of our minds. This sutra rejects that conquest of the Absolute Truth. It says that even if you attain a vision of the Lord, the Lord is not conquered; He still remains unachieved, because He has infinite aspects and we only know one of those aspects. This sutra also refers to the Absolute Truth as aviśiṣṭa which means He is not bound by our individual cultural, societal, or religious ideologies. It doesn't mean that He is *not* that vision. It just means that He is much more than that vision. It then goes on to say that the Lord is as if forever unachievable. But then one might say: If we cannot know the Lord, then why should we even try? And the answer to that is also there: The achievement and non-achievement are equivalent.

This sophisticated doctrine of the Absolute Truth rests on the second type of aspect theory in which the many aspects of the Absolute Truth are hidden inside each aspect. So, the person who sees the Lord as a father, may not see His child-like nature, but that nature exists within Him. If we get close to the Lord, then we will find that even the father is child-like, mother-like, son-like, friend-like, etc. This discovery of the Lord is an infinite process. The devotees of the Lord just get attached to one aspect of the Lord and they go to His place. Then they spend eternity discovering all His other aspects. Of course, if someone is not interested in any other aspect, then the Lord doesn't reveal them. He can always remain the father or master if one so chooses. But that doesn't mean that He is *only* the father or master. He is everything else, but it depends on who we are. Thus, if our nature changes, then the Lord also adapts to it.

This is the dance of the Lord with the devotee; as the devotee changes his or her personality, the Lord changes Himself too. So, dancing with the Lord is discovering His various aspects. Every dance move reveals a unique aspect of His persona that wasn't seen before. It is not physical dancing, which is why those who are conditioned by physical thinking are advised to refrain from reading about the Lord's dancing. The Lord's dance is a semantic dance in which the same person reveals various aspects of their personality to the willing participant. This means that we have to be willing to see the Lord in a new way.

Many devotees of the Lord are not willing in this way. They prefer to see the Lord in one specific way. So, the Lord doesn't dance with His father and mother, because they like to see the Lord in one specific manner. But the highest devotees of the Lord—the gopis—are not satisfied by only one vision. They want to see all the aspects of the Lord. So, the Lord dances with them, revealing Himself in ever new ways. This dancing is the limit of spiritual perfection. But even this dancing is limitless and eternal because no matter how many dance moves are made, the full personality of emotions, expressions, moods, and gestures is never known. So, the gopis know the Lord better than anyone. But even the gopis don't know the Lord completely: They are eagerly waiting for the next dance to discover something new. Hence, the Lord is in one sense totally bound by the love of the devotee. In another sense, He is never attained by anyone. This binding and freedom are the contradictory nature of the Infinite. The free nature is Infinite, and the bound nature is something specific. The Lord is infinite specific things, so He is both bound, and yet He is completely free.

One, Oneness, and Separateness

The following is an excerpt from the Vaiśeṣika Sutras, that describes the three principles of One, Oneness, and Separateness, which create two paradoxes—*unity in diversity* and *diversity in unity*. Many things emerge out of the One, therefore, they must have existed in the One previously; this is the paradox of diversity in the unity. Similarly, when the many things have emerged from the One, Oneness is immanent in the many things; this is the paradox of unity in the diversity. These three principles are called Bhagavān, Paramātma, and Brahman in the Bhāgavat Purāna. Bhagavān is One, Paramātma is Oneness, and Brahman is many things (which create a "space" of individual locations). One, Oneness, and Separateness are therefore general principles based on which diversity and unity are understood.

Sutra 7.2.3

एकत्वैकपृथक्त्वयोरेकत्वैकपृथक्त्वा
भावो ऽणुत्वमहत्त्वाभ्यां व्याख्यातः

ekatvaikapṛthaktvayorekatvaikapṛthaktvābhāvo
'ṇutvamahattvābhyāṃ vyākhyātaḥ

ekatva—oneness; eka—one; pṛthaktvayoh—in the separateness; ekatva—oneness; eka—one; pṛthaktva—separateness; abhāvah—absence; aṇutva—atomism; mahattvābhyāṃ–from greatness; vyākhyātaḥ–is explained.

TRANSLATION

The absence of oneness, one, and separateness in the oneness, one, and separateness is explained by atomism arising from greatness.

COMMENTARY

The sutra describes a paradox and its solution. The paradox is that there is simultaneous diversity and oneness. The existence of diversity is the absence of the oneness, and the existence of oneness is the absence of diversity. The diversity exists because the whole truth is divided into parts. And the oneness exists because the whole truth is immanent in the parts. Since both unity and diversity exist, therefore, the separateness and oneness are absent. Similarly, the "one" is transcendent to the parts, therefore, the "one" is absent from the diversity.

The "one" from which the diversity expands, comprises all the diversity, and yet, the diversity is not separated in the "one". Therefore, there is no separateness (as there is oneness), and there is no oneness (because there is diversity). Similarly, the "one" is absent from the "one" because It has the desire for self-knowledge; that desire can exist only when the "one" doesn't know itself. This desire for self-knowledge is called abhāva due to which the self misses itself and desires to unite with itself; that union creates self-knowledge.

Thus, paradoxically, there is one (the source of everything), there is diversity (or separateness), and there is unity in the diversity (the oneness). And yet, in another sense, the one is missing from the diversity and itself, the diversity is missing in the one, and unity—even though present—is apparently missing because it is not perceived in the material condition. This leads to the paradox of one, oneness, and separateness, namely that they are at once present and absent. The resolution of the paradox is that oneness counters separateness, the separateness counters oneness, and yet both are reconciled in the one. This one expands into many due to the one missing from itself; therefore, another paradox of presence and absence is created, but the paradox is resolved if we understand this "one" as a personality with the desire for self-knowledge.

Once we understand the paradox and its resolution, then we can understand the role of atomism and greatness. Greatness is the transcendent whole truth, and atomism is the immanent representation of this whole truth within all partial truths. Just like a mammal is present within a cow, and in one sense mammal is transcendent, and in another sense immanent, in the same way, the Absolute Truth is transcendent as greatness and immanent as atomism. Thus, He is both the greatest and the smallest. His immanence in everything is the unity in everything; His transcendence being divided into parts is the diversity, and His transcendental personality is the one. Thus, the Lord is inside everything, outside everything, and everything. These three realizations about the Absolute Truth are called Paramātma, Bhagavan, and Brahman, respectively. Brahman is everything; Paramātma is the immanent truth inside everything; and Bhagavan is the transcendent truth outside everything.

If we only acknowledge diversity, then there would be no unity, and there would be no origin. If we say that there is one source for everything, but that source is transcendent, then there would be no way to *know* that source from the things. Such a postulate would become indistinguishable from arbitrary hypotheses. Hence, in addition to diversity, and a single source of diversity, we must acknowledge a unity that is immanent inside the diversity. This immanent truth creates unity in diversity, and is the means to know the transcendent one: We can look deep inside anything, and know the source of everything.

Sutra 7.2.4

नःसिंख्यत्वात् कर्मगुणानां सर्वैकत्वं न वदियते

niḥ saṃkhyatvāt karmaguṇānāṃ sarvaikatvaṃ na vidyate

niḥ–without; saṃkhyatvāt—from number-like; karma—activity; guṇānāṃ–qualities; sarva—all; ekatvaṃ–unity; na–not vidyate—known.

TRANSLATION

Without being manifested from number-like, the unity of all activities and qualities cannot be known.

COMMENTARY

This sutra states the Sāñkhya position in which all qualities and activities are essentially numbers, but these numbers are meanings. Their interaction is based on the logic of meaning interaction, and their successive manifestation is the manifestation of one number from within another. Based on the nature of numbers, their manifestation and interaction can be studied scientifically. Logic and numbers are therefore applicable to the study of qualities and activities because the qualities are activities, which are themselves numbers. But these are not quantitative numbers; each number rather symbolizes a type of meaning.

Sutra 7.2.5

भ्रान्तं तत्

bhrāntaṃ tat

bhrāntaṃ–confusing; tat—that.

TRANSLATION

That (unity due to manifestation from number-like) is confusing.

COMMENTARY

In modern science, we think of the world as matter and force, not as numbers. Matter is understood in terms of its properties like mass and charge, energy, and momentum. Forces are similarly conceived as gravity, electromagnetism, etc. How can all these things be just numbers? Despite the successes of modern science and its reliance on numbers and equations, we still don't understand why mathematics can be so successful in describing the nature of reality. This confusion is the result of thinking of numbers as quantities, rather than types of meaning. Conversely, those who don't feel confused about this success, use that success to proclaim materialism when factually all that science does is numbers and equations. This sutra answers the twin confusions about why science works, as well as why materialism is false despite its success.

The answer to the question about why science works is that nature is numbers, and the equations of science treat reality as numbers. The successes of science are owed to the fact that it has gotten one idea correct—namely, that nature should be described using mathematics. By capturing some properties of the number aggregates, science has become successful. However, the aggregation of numbers doesn't necessarily produce a number that would be obtained by the addition of constituent numbers. Numbers also have complex contextual properties due to the inverted-tree like structure in which they are produced.

A number, for instance, can be treated in three ways—an object, a quality, and an activity. A number like 10 can sometimes refer to a particular individual—e.g., employee number 10. Then, it can refer to the quality of tenness. And it can refer to an activity (e.g., if numbers are used as instructions in computers). Whether a number is an object, quality, or activity cannot be determined independently of context. But since each number is some quality, activity, or object, therefore, the result of number aggregation cannot simply be obtained by the addition of numbers. Such addition amounts to adding qualities to activities to objects—which cannot be added since they are entities of different types.

Just as apples and oranges can be added to obtain the total number of fruits, but not the total number of apples or oranges, similarly, sometimes number addition works if it pertains to a more abstract concept. And sometimes it doesn't work if we think that the addition pertains to the total number of oranges or apples. As a result, modern science is a mixture of some successes and many failures. The successes are not due to materialism; they are due to the fact that reality is numbers. And the failures are due to the fact that numbers are not quantities but types. Each number, therefore, has a unique type, which includes the type of being an object, quality, or activity. The qualities, activities, and objects are further subdivided into many subtypes. And the combination of these types requires an alternative system of type combining. That system will simultaneously undermine materialism, and produce a science that is far more powerful than current science because it accounts for the typed nature of reality.

Sutra 7.2.6

एकत्वाभावाद्भक्तसि्तु न वदियते

ekatvābhāvādbhaktistu na vidyate

ekatva—unity; abhāvāt—from the absence; bhakti—attachment; tu—but; na—not; vidyate—known.

TRANSLATION

But from the absence of unity (between objects, qualities, and activities), the attachments (between them) cannot be known.

COMMENTARY

The last sutra stated that the unity between objects, qualities, and activities is very confusing, and this sutra counters—but, if we don't consider this unity then we cannot explain how these things are combined. This is the doctrine of similar things combine with similar things, and dissimilar things cannot interact. Therefore, if activities are disparate from qualities, then they cannot be produced from qualities, nor can they modify objects. Hence, even though the unity between objects, qualities, and activities is confusing, it must be accepted because the alternative makes it impossible to understand the nature of reality.

Sutra 7.2.7

कार्यकारणयोरेकत्वैकपृथक्त्वाभावादेकत्वैकपृथक्त्वं न वदियते

kāryakāraṇayorekatvaikapṛthaktvābhāvādekatvaikapṛthaktvaṃ na vidyate

kārya—effect; kāraṇayoh—and the cause; ekatva—unity; eka—one; pṛthaktva—separateness; abhāvāt—from the absence; ekatva—unity; eka—one; pṛthaktvaṃ–separateness; na—not; vidyate—known.

TRANSLATION

The oneness, unity, and separateness of cause and effect are not known from the absence of oneness, unity, and separateness.

COMMENTARY

This sutra revisits the paradox we have discussed earlier. To recall, the paradox is that (a) there is one cause for everything, (b) there are many things produced from that cause, and (c) all these varied things have unity. The last two create the paradox of *unity in diversity*, and the first two create the paradox of *diversity in the unity*. If diversity did not exist in the unity, then many things could not be created from that unity. Similarly, if unity did not exist in the diversity, then the many produced things could not interact with each other.

The previous sutras have elaborated on the nature of the unity—namely, that they are all numbers, and hence they can combine and interact. But this unity is qualitative—we are talking about the property of numerosity and then treating all the individual numbers as the subclasses of that numerosity. If we remove either of the above three—oneness, unity, and separateness—then we cannot explain (a) the single source for everything, (b) many manifested things, and (c) the basis for interaction between these things. Thus, a pure singularity of cause doesn't work because it leads to only one effect, rather than many effects. A pure plurality of causes and effects doesn't work because we cannot explain why these things are able to interact with each other without a similarity, which requires a single source of causation. Hence, by removing any one of these three principles of unity, oneness, and separateness, we lose the basis for all three.

How Vaiśeṣika Explains the Immune System

Cognition and Adaptation in Disease

The world is today gripped by the CoVID pandemic. Every few days new vaccines and virus variants are talked about. The governments are pressured into vaccination, the doctors have no time (and limited ability) to test if a person is already immune to CoVID before administering a vaccine. And nobody can say if a vaccine creates immunity against the new variants. All these problems can be debated at the level of politics, but that's not what I will do here. I will try to describe fundamental flaws in the modern understanding of matter, and why that understanding creates difficulties in describing the cognitive and adaptive abilities in the immune system, leading to numerous other downstream problems.

The Cartesian Mind-Body Divide

The problem begins in the Cartesian mind-body divide. The mind has capacities for recognition, but matter doesn't. Why? Because "knowledge" is in the mind, and matter only works due to "force". Similarly, the mind has the capacity for adaptation to new questions or problems, but matter doesn't. Matter only acts due to blind forces; it doesn't react selectively or differently to a "problem". Why? Because matter has no problem. Problems only exist for the minds, not for matter. The mind wants to solve problems, but matter has no such purpose. Without a purpose, there cannot be an adaptation.

This dogma incarnates in biology in the doctrine of genes. Your immune response requires some unique proteins and the gene codes for all possible proteins. If there is a gene encoding for the protein, then you have immunity against a certain disease. Otherwise, not. Since the genetic markers are fixed at birth, you are predestined to be non-immune to the diseases for which the proteins are not encoded (unless, of course, you are immunized against that disease).

Now, contrast this claim to how we solve day-to-day problems—by recognition and adaptation. If you don't have the best tools in your toolbox of solutions, then you have two choices. First, you can create the tool best suited to solve the problem, and then use it. Second, you can use a combination of existing tools to solve the problem, although the solution may be less effective. The fact that you don't have a unique tool suite for a specific problem doesn't prevent you from solving those problems. And the reason is that you recognize the problem, devise a new tool, or combine existing tools to solve the problem. This is what I mean by "recognition" and "adaptation" to problems.

When the body is described as a machine, then it cannot have capacities for recognition and adaptation. It must rather already be preprogrammed with some tools to solve problems. There must be specificity between tools and problems, and new combinations of existing tools cannot be created, because the specificity of the problem and tool is predetermined. Likewise, there is no ability to create new tools, because the so-called genetic markers have preprogrammed all the possible tools.

How the Cartesian Divide Impacts Immunology

The Cartesian divide explicitly removes from the study of matter the mental capacity for solving problems by recognition of the problem and the adaptation of the tools to solve it. The real meaning of the mind-body divide is that matter cannot have recognition and adaptation.

Now the fact that the immune system has cognitive and adaptive capacities must be paradigmatically outside the study of matter. At least, it requires additional capacities of recognition and adaptation, which cannot in principle be reduced to matter, and without those capacities, there is no immunity. All immunity now reduces to vaccination—you must be given what you don't have through an injection.

The problem is that the number of potential diseases is infinite. How many times, and for what things, must you be injected? Why does the body not have the capacity for recognition and adaptation, when even by evolutionary accounts, this presents a far greater evolutionary advantage? But the issue is that we don't know how to reduce adaptation and recognition to molecules. While we can see that all immune systems are capable of handling millions of disease variants, they do fail sometimes. Why they fail is erroneously attributed to a missing tool, ignoring the fact that in other cases of disease resistance, a combination of tools is used, and in some cases, entirely new tools are created in real-time.

The genetic dogma now says: Let's inject the tools into the system, to help it solve a new problem. Thus, the fundamental questions about the cognitive and adaptive nature of the immune system are neglected. The fact that we don't have the capability to understand these are seldom recognized.

The Vaiśeṣika Description of Matter

I will now turn to summarize the Vaiśeṣika understanding of material interactions. For those who don't know, the Vaiśeṣika system is the Vedic philosophical system that describes the nature of atoms.

Without getting into too much detail (I'm writing a commentary on the Vaiśeṣika Sutras, which should be out sometime later this year), the Vaiśeṣika process comprises of the following four steps:

- Matter exists in a state of potentiality, and everything that exists potentially is not always visible. It rather becomes visible when that potentiality is subjected to a problem.
- Material objects interact with other objects to create a "knowledge" of the external reality within themselves. A picture of the external world is produced internally by an interaction.

- Once the external reality is pictured within, it is sometimes recognized as a problem. This problem is called the "absence" (or something is missing). It is a state begging for a solution.
- Once the problem is created within, one of the many states from the states of preexisting potentialities is selected as a solution. This selection of potentiality becomes an "activity".

The first step of these four steps is recognized in modern atomic theory, where matter is said to exist as potentials. But how that potential "collapses" into reality is unknown. Vaiśeṣika answers that question: The potential collapses into a solution when it is subjected to a problem. Then, the potential is the solution to a problem. If the problem doesn't arise, then the potential remains a potentiality.

However, this solution to the quantum measurement problem also requires us to understand how the external world is "represented" inside as "knowledge", and how that "knowledge" is then recognized as a "problem", and how that problem then selects a preexisting tool from the toolkit of potential answers to produce an "activity". All these require us to treat matter as meaning—and therefore mind-like—rather than matter in a Cartesian sense. If we cannot treat matter in that way, we can never solve the collapse problem. And if we cannot solve that problem, then everything seems to occur randomly.

The difference between Vaiśeṣika and modern materialism is subtle but important. In materialism, matter acts according to force—which applies to all things, everywhere, all the time. In Vaiśeṣika, matter acts depending on a problem—which applies if the problem appears, selectively in relation to that problem, only where the problem exists, and only when the problem appears. In simple terms, in Vaiśeṣika, matter is already "intelligent"—adaptive, cognitive, and responsive to problems.

The Application of Vaiśeṣika to Problems of Immunity

Now, we can use this basic understanding of Vaiśeṣika to understand its application to immunity.

- Immunity exists in everyone as a potentiality. What that potential is, is not always visible because that potentiality has not yet been subjected to a question or a problem.
- When a disease enters a body—say a virus or bacteria—the cell creates an information representation or "knowledge" of the world internally. This is a picture of reality.
- This "knowledge" is now processed to determine that there is a problem. This problem now creates an "absence" which is the preliminary step to solving the problem.
- The problem or "absence" scans and interacts with the pre-existing potentiality to identify a solution. That potential is activated and that is when potentiality becomes "activity".

Thus, to understand immunity, we should use a different language comprising of words such as potentiality, knowledge, problem, and activity. We cannot superimpose this language on the world of atoms and molecules, because an atom is never knowledge, problem, or solution. It is sometimes a possibility, and then a reality. The mechanism of "collapse" of possibility to reality is absent because the mechanism requires knowledge representation, problem recognition, and solution selection, which can never be attained through the physical properties. It requires matter to be semantic.

The Truth in Immunology and Its Limitations

Since immunity exists as a potentiality, it is quite possible that different individuals have different potentials. When a person is injected with a vaccine, it is the injection of new knowledge into the system, which then alters the potentiality, which then lies dormant unless a new disease appears. Thus, immunization has a basis even if we accept the Vaiśeṣika principles—it adds knowledge to the system.

But this doesn't end the discourse. There are three other questions. First, why could this knowledge not have been acquired through other means? Or, more precisely, why does it exist in some individuals and not in others? Second, why could it not have been derived from preexisting knowledge? Surely, the novelty in a new disease is very small; the commonalities with the other diseases are huge. Third, why could a set of preexisting tools not be adapted for application to the new problem? Sure, they may be slightly more complex and slower, but are they really so novel to resist any existing solution?

Immunology ignores these questions and settles quickly on identifying a vaccine. This has more to do with the business models of medicine than with the understanding of biology and medication.

Classical systems of medicine have always focused on the three questions not addressed by immunology. For example, if person X has immunity against disease and Y doesn't, then what were the key differences in the X's lifestyle, food habits, mental states, and other such factors, compared to Y? By identifying these differences, they are also able to prescribe cures, in which knowledge is injected into a system, but that knowledge is *generic* in nature, rather than *specific* to a particular disease.

Just like by acquiring an understanding of some natural theory, we are able to solve a wide variety of problems, but if you are given a complicated machine, you can solve a fewer number of problems.

The difference in knowledge is with regard to its nature—abstract and general vs. detailed and specific. The classical systems of medicine focus on providing abstract and general information, which is then combined with the preexisting information to produce adequate responses to a wide variety of immune problems. The modern systems of medicine focus on providing detailed and specific information, which is then used to solve a very specific problem, which proves ineffective for other cases. Indeed, in some cases, it might interact with other knowledge, and destroy the immunity for other diseases.

Classical Medicine is Based on Qualities

Classical medicine studied matter as qualities. These qualities were described in terms of their taste, smell, touch, color, form, etc. When a disease was identified, it was traced to the absence of a certain quality, which was compensated by the consumption of different foods and natural herbs. These foods and herbs then created the missing quality. In short, immunization was replaced by food and herbs as the source of missing information or qualities due to a person's differing lifestyle, habits, etc.

Once these qualities were naturally acquired and assimilated, they acted as abstract information, which can be used to solve a wide variety of problems, not limited to that specific disease. Since that knowledge has now disappeared, and the study of matter is based on physical quantities rather than perceptual qualities, therefore, the scientific basis of classical medicine has also declined. It is not extinct, however. Its application requires the revival of a qualitative study of matter.

Should You Vaccinate or Not?

I'm sure many of you might be eager to jump to an answer to some practical things you can do. Unfortunately, there is no easy answer to this question, because there is no comparative study of people who had immunity and who had not, and the differences between lifestyle, food habits, and mental states between these two groups. Without that comparative study—which is quickly preempted in favor of immunization—there is not enough data to identify the correct classical medicine.

So, I cannot provide you an answer regarding vaccination, one way or another. But I can tell you what the problem is, why it arises due to the dogmas of modern science, which then incarnate in medicine, what their solution is, and how that solution differs from the currently prevalent solutions. That recipe for solving problems is also knowledge, but it must be cooked in practice before you can consume it.

CREATION AS CONSCIOUS CREATIVITY

Beginning with my first book, "Six Causes", I have been describing a paradigm of creation that stems from conscious creativity. In this paradigm, the self goes missing in the self, and when this "absence" is created, then creativity occurs to overcome this absence by expanding the self into works of creativity. E.g. in human creativity, the person who desires to know himself expands into products such as art, music, literature, poetry, and science. All those things that expand out of the self, were previously in the self. And once those things have expanded, they are used to define the creator, author, musician, artist, or scientist. The work of an artist is not the artist, but art is used to define the artist. By externalizing himself as art, the artist knows himself. The artist is transcendent to the work of art and yet immanent in the art.

But readers often ask: "Where did you get this idea from?" They are generally looking for a reference from the Purānas, Upaniśads, etc. but this idea is not directly found in these texts, although its implications (e.g., that the creator is transcendent and immanent) are described.

This idea is a core aspect of the Six Systems of Philosophy. For example, in the Vedānta Sutra, the creation is said to be the Lord's *abhivyakti* which means "expressing the self". Similarly, in Nyāya and Vaiśeṣika, the doctrine of "absence" that leads to a "presence" (abhāva and bhāva) is discussed extensively. Here, I will reproduce a few verses from the Sāñkhya Sūtras to illustrate the same idea.

Topic 20

प्रकृतेरेव सर्वजगन्मूलत्वं

prakṛtereva sarvajaganmūlatvaṃ
Prakṛti is the Root of Everything in the World

Sūtra 1.67
मूले मूलाभावादमूलं मूलं
mūle mūlābhāvādamūlaṃ mūlaṃ

mūle—in the root; mūla—the root; abhāvāt—due to the absence; amūlaṃ—that which is not the root; mūlaṃ—that which is the root.

TRANSLATION

Due to the absence of the root in the root, that which is not the root is the root.

COMMENTARY

To understand this sūtra, which describes the process of material creation, we can visualize how creativity works in us. We exist, but everybody asks: Who am I? This is because we are incomplete. We want to define and know ourselves better because the self is missing within the self. When this need to define the self is produced within us, then from the self we create numerous products—e.g., works of art, poetry, literature, music, and science—which are all creations out of the self, and yet, by creating them we define ourselves: "I am the creator of such creations, and therefore, now, I am well-defined by my creation".

Thus, creation is created by the process of creativity, and in that process, there is a need for someone to know themselves, because the self is missing in the self. When the self creates some products, then those products are distinct from the self, and yet, those products are used to define the self. For instance, a poet's poetry is not the poet; and yet, the poetry defines the poet. Hence, that which is not the self (i.e., the poetry) becomes the defining trait of the self.

We can extend this idea to concepts such as a mammal and a cow. The mammal is the root, from which the cow is manifest. But why should a cow manifest from the mammal? The answer is that mammal is not well-defined unless all the types of mammals—e.g., cow, horse, dog, cat, etc.—are defined. The mammal is an abstract idea, and it is well-defined by presenting the details. These details can include the fact that mammals can be two-legged or four-legged; that they can be tall or short; that they can have various colors and sizes, etc. Thus, the cow manifests from the mammal in an attempt to completely define the mammal. And after the manifestation, the mammal is not the cow, but the cow is a mammal. Why? Because the mammal still exists as a separate thing, but the definition of cow becomes one of the ways in which the mammal is defined. There are other ways too: E.g., a dog is also a mammal. Thus, the concept mammal cannot be equated either to the dog or the cow; the mammal is separate from them. And yet, both dogs and cows are the ways in which a mammal is defined.

This paradox of the self being absent from the self to produce something which is not the self, and yet defines the self, is the principle of conscious creativity and it is used as the description of creation all over Vedic philosophy. This basic process of absence, which is called abhāva, is also used in Nyāya and Vaiśeṣika. These latter two philosophies delve a great deal deeper into the various kinds of absences, how different kinds of things are created from absence. For example, an object—e.g., a knife—has qualities such as shape and size and activities such as piercing and cutting. However, these qualities and activities are not simultaneously manifest. Their occasional manifestation requires a context of observation and use, which is when the 'unmanifest' is 'manifest'.

Now, the proposal seems relatively straightforward if we say that something external triggers a potentiality. For example, we can say that a table has a mass, which is manifest if we try to measure that mass; here, the procedure of measurement is the trigger, and the quality of heaviness is manifest due to that trigger. The same process seems harder if we say that something is manifest automatically from within the same thing because the question is: What is the trigger? Of course, we could ask the same question even in the case of measuring weight. Why should we measure weight? And the answer is that we don't *know* something's weight, and therefore, a measurement is performed to overcome that incompleteness. The same principle is then applied even in the case of self-manifestation—we don't know who we are, and we create products such as art, music, literature, poetry, and science, merely to define who we are. Or, that the mammal is not well-defined so it manifests a cow to define itself.

Once the created product has manifest, then each piece of art, each poem, each theory of science, each musical composition, and each essay, contains the author's personality: We say that this is the author's work because there is a unique trait or aspect of the author embedded in the art, poem, music, science, or essay. And yet, because there are so many works of art, poetry, music, etc., therefore, the author of these works is not identical to the works. Hence, we are compelled to say that "the art is the artist, but the artist is not the art". We could also say the opposite: "the artist is the art, but the art is not the artist". This is because there is an artist separate from the art, but the artist is defined by the art, and without the art, the artist remains incomplete or undefined.

These twin premises are commonly used to say that a dog is a mammal, but a mammal is not a dog. The property of being a mammal is immanent in the dog, but the property of the mammal is also transcendent to the dog, cow, cat, horse, etc. The paradox, therefore, is that the mammal is *both* immanent and transcendent; the artist is immanent in the work of art, and yet, transcendent to the work of art. That work of art came out since the artist missed himself, and when the work of art was produced, then the artist was embedded in the art. By embedding himself in the art, the artist defines himself through the art.

Sūtra 1.68

पारम्पयैऽपि एकत्र परिनिष्ठेति संज्ञामात्रं

pārampayai'pi ekatra parinișțheti saṃjñāmātraṃ

pārampaya—subsequently; api—even; ekatra—all these together; parinișțh—joined together, iti—thus; saṃjñāmātraṃ—merely nouns.

TRANSLATION

Subsequently, even all these together which are joined (to the root) are thus merely nouns or ways of knowing (by which the root is called or known).

COMMENTARY

All the mammals, such cows, horses, dogs, etc. are merely ways of understanding the mammal, and by knowing these species, we know the nature of the mammal. In the same way, when the root has expanded, all the expansions are different ways of knowing the root. The term saṃjñā means a name, a noun, or the way of knowing the thing. All these meanings are easily understood when we realize that cows, dogs, horses, etc. are just varieties of mammals.

Similarly, all the works of art, poetry, literature, science, and music, are merely the ways of knowing a person. Those things came out of the person; therefore, they were previously embedded within the person and were subsequently externalized. It is impossible to know the person unless he externalizes himself in the form of some art, literature, poetry, science, or music. But if those creations are externalized, then the artist is known *through* those creations. Those creations are not the creator, but they are methods of knowing him. Since they define the creator, therefore, they are the various aspects of the creator, and yet, the creator—as the collection of all those aspects—is distinct from them. Hence, this sutra states that these creations are merely nouns to know the creator. By the creation, the creator gets many names, but those names are the creator in one sense, and yet, the creator is distinct from all those names.

Sūtra 1.69

समाजःप्रकृतेर्द्वयोः

samājaḥ prakṛterdvayoḥ

samājaḥ—the same unborn; prakṛti—the prakṛti; dvayoḥ—the duality.

TRANSLATION

The same unborn prakṛti is the duality (of the various names).

COMMENTARY

All the elements of Sāñkhya are produced as the various manifestations of prakṛti, by the process of defining the prakṛti. Thus, in the primordial state called pradhāna, there is an absence: What do we *mean* by pradhāna? This leads to the first answer when prakṛti is manifest. Then the next question arises: What do we mean by prakṛti? This is answered when mahattattva is manifest. In this way, through successive questions and answers, there is an expansion, until we come to the point where the questions cease. Thus, in the final element called Earth, the question "What is Earth?" doesn't arise, and therefore, there is no further manifestation. In the Śrīmad Bhāgavatām, it is stated that all the elements are present in the Earth. Why? This is because the abstract entity is immanent in the contingent entity, just like a mammal (an abstract entity) is immanent in the cow (a contingent entity). Therefore, Water is immanent in Earth, and since Fire is immanent in Water, therefore, Fire is also immanent in the Earth. Likewise, the source of everything—namely, the Supreme Lord—is immanent in everything as Paramātma. Thus, the source of everything expands into numerous things, so long as the question "What is this?" doesn't end. Since questioning has similarities to the conscious process of creativity, therefore, all the elements other than the Earth are just like conscious beings, although with diminishing power of questioning. The Earth element seems to be totally inert because it doesn't ask the question underlying creativity: What am I?

All of classical physics was developed based on the study of the Earth element, without actually studying its true properties—i.e., smell, taste, sight, touch, and sound. Rather, all these properties were reduced to a simple concept of 'particle' with 'mass'. We can ask: Why does classical physics work? And the answer is: Because the property of consciousness—i.e., What am I?—is absent in it. This absence was falsely interpreted to mean that matter is separate from the mind, that it exists eternally, rather than being manifest out of a process of conscious creativity. Thus, a fact about Earth is universalized into a doctrine about all matter, and a false doctrine of material nature is produced. We can also ask: Why does Earth not have the urge to know itself? Surely, if that urge existed, then Earth would further manifest into other elements. And the answer is that this urge is originally from a conscious person—the Lord's Sakti—and the nature of consciousness defines the nature of matter. That is, there is a limit to the urge in consciousness, and there is no notion of a perceptual quality besides taste, touch, smell, sound, and sight. Hence, when all these questions are answered, then, the questioning comes to an end, and Earth seems inert. That inertness is also a property of consciousness—the end of questioning—when all the questions have been satisfied. Hence, if we begin with consciousness, then we can explain inertness; but if we begin with inertness, then we cannot explain consciousness. The method from consciousness to matter, therefore, works to explain the nature of 'inert' matter, but the reverse process does not work.

Once we understand this process, then we can understand the meaning of non-duality stated in this sutra. The more abstract element contains all the contingent manifestations that are produced from it, but they are not separated in the abstract element. For instance, if an author produces 5 books, then in his mind, those books don't exist as separate compartments or boxes of information. What exists instead is *knowledge* from which the books were previously manifest as aspects of that knowledge. Each book is an aspect, which is separate—if you look at them as books—but they were earlier present in the author's mind in a non-separated form. These books also don't exist as the precise words which were subsequently encoded in the book's text. In the author's mind, there is no separation of ideas into chapters, sections, paragraphs, and sentences. This separation is a byproduct of the process of manifestation. Thereby, a huge amount of information is added. But that information was previously *compressed* as knowledge in the author. Thus, the expansion of the universe is the expansion of something that was earlier compressed. The difference is just that the compression is semantic, rather than physical. That is, all the books are not zipped as compressed files in the author's brain (if you think of the brain as a storage disk). They are rather compressed as semantic information, in which only the ideas are stored, and sentences are discarded.

Thus, non-duality is the same as semantic abstraction and compression, and duality is the same as the separation of information into individual aspects by expansion. We just have to understand semantic rather than physical compression and expansion, and the concepts of duality and non-duality will be clear.

The Mīmāṃsā Doctrine of Arthavāda

All over Vedic texts, the world is described as "sound" or "text". The source of this world is stated to be the original meaning, called "knowledge". This original meaning then expands to create various other types of meanings, which are all partial knowledge.

The Mīmāṃsā system of philosophy gives this doctrine a name–Arthavāda–or the doctrine of meaning. I often use the term "semanticism" instead. The following selection from Mīmāṃsā Sutras gives a glimpse into various aspects of this doctrine of meaning, such as

- Mantras are universal meanings,
- Material objects are representations of these meanings,
- All computation in nature occurs based on these meanings,
- This semantic view of reality is the basis on which atheism is rejected,
- On this basis the possibility of a textual representation of the truth is established,
- The principle of unity in diversity is established by this meaning,
- The Vedic texts being the truth as they establish the unity in diversity is proven.

The following few Sutras cover this enormous ground and illustrate the nature of semanticism.

Sūtra 1.2.40

अवशिष्टस् तु वाक्यार्थः

aviśiṣṭas tu vākyārthaḥ

aviśiṣṭah—the non-specific; tu—but; vākyārthaḥ—meaning of statements.

TRANSLATION

The meaning of mantra statements is but non-specific or universals.

COMMENTARY

This sūtra clarifies that chanting of mantras gives us the aviśiṣṭa. The term viśiṣṭa refers to the individual things which are instantiations of ideas. Likewise, it refers to the leaves and twigs of the tree of knowledge, instead of the roots. Thereby, the term aviśiṣṭa refers to the universal ideas and the abstract ideas. By the chanting of these mantras, the mind acquires these abstract and universal ideas. These ideas are the pure and perfect forms, and many mantras are presented in Vedic texts to gradually elevate a person from the contingent to the abstract, and from the individual to the universal. Since these universals are organized in a hierarchy, there are many levels of mantras—some more advanced than others. Those who have seen the forms of contingent ideas mentally can practice the mantras that depict the abstract forms. The goal of the mantra is never to obtain individual material instances of the ideas (e.g., some instance of wealth, power, beauty, health, etc.). It is rather to understand the abstract ideas—i.e., what do we *mean* by health, wealth, beauty, or power? These ideas have pure forms which are illuminated by the mantra chanting. If such pure ideas are obtained, then even the instances of these ideas are judged correctly. For instance, grains, milk, land, and jewels are understood as far superior types of wealth than paper money, stock market paper, or government bonds. Likewise, one understands the true meaning of beauty, the perfect use of power, and the correct way to obtain a healthy body and mind, and so on.

Sūtra 1.2.41

गुणार्थेन पुनःश्रुतिः

guṇārthena punaḥ śrutiḥ

guṇārthena—by the meaning of material qualities; punaḥ—repeated; śrutiḥ—so says the śrutī.

TRANSLATION

(The non-specific or universals) are repeated by the meaning of material qualities, so says the śrutī.

COMMENTARY

The mantras are called śabda-brahman and the material objects are called artha-brahman. They are related as words and meaning. The word represents the universal, and when someone chants the mantra, there are individual instances of that universal in their mind. The mantra—as a statement—is, therefore, a universal that embodies the idea, and the chanting of the mantra is the instance of that universal. Likewise, the material nature encodes the same idea. Of course, the material nature also elaborates that idea in greater detail whereas the idea is summarized in the mantra and our mind. Thus, the two meanings of aviśiṣṭa as abstract and universal are converted into their opposites—detailed and individual—by the material modes. We can call the mantra summarized information and the world detailed information. The world can be manipulated by injecting summarized information just as altering the instructions in a computer program changes the working of the computer. This creates a new kind of technology where the world is altered, controlled, and organized just by utterances. However, as we have noted, this is not the primary goal of the mantras; the primary goal is the purification of the mind. When the primary goal is abandoned, then the mantras stop working as the quality of chanting declines.

Sūtra 1.2.42
परिसंख्या
parisaṃkhyā

parisaṃkhyā—calculation.

TRANSLATION

Calculation (is based on the non-specific or universals).

COMMENTARY

Numbers in modern thinking are quantities, but to count we need the ability to distinguish, identify, and order things. For instance, to count to apples, we must draw a boundary around each apple, then identify that boundary as being of the type apple, and then select one apple ahead of the other. The quantity is the byproduct of distinguishing, identifying, and ordering. The Vedic system assigns numerosity to the cause—i.e., the concepts that assist the distinguishing, ordering, and counting—while the modern system assigns numerosity to the effects—i.e., the quantity. Accordingly, the calculations in the Vedic system pertain to the concepts, which are called non-specific universals. Each number in this view is a meaning and the combinations of numbers are also meanings. The rules of combination pertain to the meanings, or elementary meanings are combined to produce complex meanings. Similarly, even the calculation of material properties involves the use of the same universals. Therefore, we could also say that the calculation is based on the modes of nature.

Sūtra 1.2.43
अर्थवादो वा
arthavādo vā

arthavādah—the doctrine of meaning; vā—alternatively.

TRANSLATION

Alternatively, this is the doctrine of meaning or semantics.

COMMENTARY

In Vedic philosophy, material reality is a text, and descriptions of reality are also text. A text has the property of being able to refer to another text. For instance, we could say "that sentence is false", in which "that" refers to another sentence. Similarly, our minds are texts, that can refer to other minds, other things, or other sentences. Thus, everything is meaningful, because everything is text. It can be true or false meaning, but it always exists as some text. This is the broader doctrine of semantics which is called arthavāda in this sūtra. This sūtra identifies with that doctrine and establishes the equivalence of previous sutras (which noted universals or aviśiṣṭa and individuals or viśiṣṭa, followed by the calculation based on these universals and individuals) with arthavāda.

Sūtra 1.2.44
अविरुद्धं परम्
aviruddhaṃ param

aviruddhaṃ—not opposed; param—the supreme truth.

TRANSLATION

(The doctrine of arthavāda) is not opposed to the supreme truth.

COMMENTARY

Modern atheism is the result of treating reality as physical entities that exist but have no meaning. This meaning takes three forms—concept, context, and purpose. Each thing is associated with a concept or a universal, as that thing is the instance of that universal. This concept also acquires additional contextual properties which are attributable to the role the object is playing. And the universal is instantiated with a certain purpose, and therefore, it has some unique properties that are not part of the universal. Modern science strips the world of these meanings. When the meaning is removed, life becomes purposeless. With the removal of purpose, choices are denied, and with that rejection, the soul—as the source of choices—is denied. Then God is also rejected because the soul was earlier rejected. The sequence of steps that lead to atheism, therefore, begins in the non-semantic view about matter. If matter is understood semantically, then all successive steps that lead to atheism will also be disproved.

This sūtra notes that the semantic doctrine is not opposed to the idea of the supreme truth, which means that one may not be devoted to God, but one cannot deny God's existence. Materialism, in contrast, is fundamentally opposed to God's existence (even though some materialists have tried to superimpose the idea of God upon materialism, and continue to do that even to this day).

Sūtra 1.2.45

संप्रैषे करमगरहानुपालम्भःसंस्कारत्त्वात्

saṃpraiṣe karmagarhānupālambhaḥ saṃskārattvāt

saṃpraiṣe—in the sacrificial invitation; karma—actions; garhān—censure; upālambhaḥ—prohibition; saṃskārattvāt—due to the purifying impressions.

TRANSLATION

Due to the purifying impressions (created) in the sacrificial invitation, the censure of actions is prohibited.

COMMENTARY

Vedic texts often talk about ending the cycle of birth and death. They state that this cycle is created by our actions. These actions in turn arise from desires. We cannot desire what we don't know about. We desire what we are familiar with. This means that the world creates impressions in us, and then we desire them. This perpetuates the cycle of impressions, desires, and actions. To end the cycle of birth and death, therefore, a common injunction is to end the impressions which will then create desires in us. This injunction is upheld by the renunciates who talk about abandoning the world and getting self-absorbed. They say that worldly action binds us to the cycle of birth and death. The endeavor for liberation requires us to end this cycle giving up worldly action.

This sūtra however rejects this conclusion. It states that sacrificial actions do not fall into the category of actions binding a person to the world because they create purifying impressions. Even if we desire those impressions again, we will be desiring more purification. The cause of repeated cycle of birth and death is desire for impure impressions. Thus, there are pure and impure actions and the pure actions are liberating while the impure actions are binding.

The renunciation of action only pertains to the binding actions. Sacrificial performances are not causes of bondage. Hence, their renunciation is forbidden by this sūtra. Thus, after stating in the previous sūtra that Arthavāda is not opposed to the supreme truth, this sūtra states that it can assist the attainment of supreme truth, if the purpose of the actions is also supreme truth. Since everyone may not act with the supreme purpose, therefore, their actions can be binding. But this is not a fault of Arthavāda itself. Arthavāda is simply saying that the world is meaningful. It is not saying that all meaning is the supreme truth. Thus, through Arthavāda we can understand both binding and liberating actions. If the purpose is supreme, then the action is liberating, otherwise, not.

Sūtra 1.2.46

अभिधानेऽर्थवादः

abhidhāne'rthavādaḥ

abhidhāne—in the teaching; arthavādaḥ—of arthavāda.

TRANSLATION

(The refutation of the objections to Vedic instructions about actions) are in the teaching of arthavāda.

COMMENTARY

This sūtra expands the scope of Arthavāda and states that it is not merely a doctrine about reality, but also one that defeats any doctrine of inaction. We can also include in this refutation any other rejection of meaningful actions given in the Vedic texts. Many people are fond of calling ritualistic actions mythology or mumbo-jumbo because they don't know that meaning resides in the action. Some actions create purifying impressions while others create impure impressions. The former lead to ascent and the latter to descent. Thus, we judge the actions by their uplifting and downgrading effects. Those who talk about inaction cannot create purifying impressions and they will be dragged down by former impure impressions. Those who talk about the meaninglessness of all actions will still not create purifying impressions and will be dragged down by the impure impressions. Thus, Arthavāda has two roles—(a) clarify the role playing by meaningful impressions, and (b) use that to establish why the Vedic texts prescribe certain types of purificatory processes for our upliftment.

Sūtra 1.2.47

गुणाद् अप्रतषिधःस्यात्

guṇād apratiṣedhaḥ syāt

guṇāt—due to qualities; apratiṣedhaḥ—non-opposition; syāt—possibility.

TRANSLATION

(By arthavāda) there is the possibility of non-opposition due to qualities.

COMMENTARY

All over Vedic texts, the material qualities are described as hindrances to the attainment of the supreme truth. But this sūtra states that there is a possibility of removal of these hindrances by the doctrine of Arthavāda. How? The answer is that these material qualities instantiate universals. Therefore, if these qualities become reflections of the supreme truth, then they are not hindrances.

The material world can be viewed as a thing or as a picture. If it is viewed as a thing, then it becomes a source of bondage. But if it is seen as picture, then we can ask: What is it a picture of? Again, it could be a picture of purity or impurity. If it is a picture of purity, then a transcendent reality is reflected in the picture. If instead the world is seen as a thing, then the questions about transcendence don't arise. Thus, a picture is a thing, but a thing is not a picture. The picture-view of reality doesn't reject the reality of the world, but it gives it meaning. Semanticism thus leads us from this world to another world. If instead the world is viewed as a thing, then it doesn't lead us to a transcendent reality. Again, the journey from the mundane to the transcendent is a possibility and not a necessity. Some people can theoretically accept that the world is a reflection of the transcendent, and still remain disinterested in the transcendent.

Sūtra 1.2.48

वदि्यावचनम् असंयोगात्

vidyāvacanam asaṃyogāt

vidyāvacanam—statements of knowledge; asaṃyogāt—due to disparate.

TRANSLATION

Due to the disparate statements of knowledge (arthavāda is necessary).

COMMENTARY

After stating the benefits of Arthavāda (namely, that by it we establish the distinction between liberating and binding actions), this sūtra states that the seemingly contradictory Vedic statements cannot be understood without Arthavāda. For example, the same supreme truth is said to be all-pervading as well as localized. Just as the concept cow is a specific form, and yet, it pervades in all cows, similarly, the supreme truth is localized and all-pervading.

A physical entity cannot be both all-pervading and localized, but a semantic entity can be both. Similarly, many contradictions in the Vedic statements are perceived when reality is conceived physically, but these contradictions disappear when we adopt a semantic understanding of reality. Hence, such an understanding is necessary even to understand the diverse Vedic statements.

Sūtra 1.2.49

सतःपरमविज्ञानम्

sataḥ paramavijñānam

sataḥ—the eternal truth; paramavijñānam—is supreme knowledge.

TRANSLATION

The eternal truth is supreme knowledge.

COMMENTARY

After stating that the understanding of Vedas depends on semanticism, this sūtra states that the supreme truth is also a meaning. That meaning pervades everything, and yet, it is localized. The localized entity has a form because it is a meaning. And the all-pervading entity also has a form, although it is present within each individual thing. Thus, the supreme truth should not be viewed as a thing, but as an idea. That idea is 'supreme knowledge'. Ordinary knowledge is divided into many departments such as mathematics, physics, chemistry, biology, psychology, sociology, economics, etc. All these are knowledge, but knowledge is not physics or chemistry. In that sense, the idea 'knowledge' is present in each department of knowledge, but 'knowledge itself' is beyond all these departments. The term 'supreme knowledge' refers to that transcendent idea which each department of knowledge reflects partially. All the departments of knowledge therefore collectively form a picture of knowledge. That supreme knowledge is present in each department, but not equal to that department. Since physics is knowledge, but knowledge is not physics, therefore, the supreme knowledge is beyond all the individual types of knowledge. This knowledge is also a form and meaning, and hence by the reconciliation of various Vedic statements, we begin to understand the nature of knowledge itself.

Sūtra 1.2.50

उक्तश् चानित्यसंयोगः

uktaś cānityasaṃyogaḥ

uktah—stated; ca—also; anitya—temporary; saṃyogaḥ—the union.

TRANSLATION

(The supreme knowledge) is stated to be the union of the temporary.

COMMENTARY

After noting that semanticism is necessary to reconcile the disparate Vedic statements and that the supreme truth is also knowledge, this sūtra states that this supreme truth is the union of the diversity of the temporary world. However, this union is conceived semantically rather than physically. For example, if different fields of knowledge such as physics, chemistry, psychology, sociology, economics, etc. cover different domains of experience and embody different kinds of ideas, then the supreme truth is that which combines all these ideas into a single and coherent understanding of reality. Similarly, if there is diversity imbued with duality—e.g., beauty is poor and power is unjust—then the union of these qualities is the perfect truth because it combines all ideas.

Modern science also tries to unify the diversity by formulating a single theory, idea, or understanding of reality but in all cases, it is far from obtaining such union. Every field of modern science is riddled with contradictions between theories that are individually successful in explaining some limited domain of experience. Similarly, there are numerous contradictions between these varied fields of science. If we put all these fields of knowledge together, along the individually successful theories within them, then we will find hundreds of contradictions between them. These contradictions, as already noted, are also present in the Vedic texts. However, Arthavāda resolves these contradictions. Therefore, the supreme truth is conceived in a scientific sense as the reconciliation of diverse domains of experience, and neither as the rejection of this experience nor as the acceptance of contradictions in explaining diverse experiences. By recognizing the diversity of experience, this doctrine is realist. But by recognizing only that idea, theory, or meaning which unites all the types of experiences into a single understanding, it is quite different from present materialistic doctrines. Hence, this type of realism is also semantic, and not physical.

When reality is conceived as meaning, judgments of truth are based on the truthfulness of meaning, rather than merely the evidence of existence. For instance, false books can exist, and their existence doesn't prove their truth. Likewise, the observability of something is only evidence of its existence, not its truth. All these things are also temporary. The truth is that which exists eternally. Likewise, the supreme truth becomes the source of all this (true and false) diversity, and the diversity appears by the division of the supreme truth.

In short, if the supreme truth is the combination of all semantic variety, then it is the cause of the variety by separating things from the combination. Quite simply, the opposites of this world—such as beauty without wealth or wealth without beauty—are the results of the separation of wealth and the byproducts of the separation of meanings from the supreme truth. This separation leads to contradictions, which are also called duality, but the union of all these dualities is non-dual. Finally, the goal of life is the attainment of perfect unity. In a mundane sense, any truth that is not beautiful is not as true as the beautiful truth. But to the extent that such dualities are only imaginable in the material world, and possible only in a transcendent sense, the goal of life is transcendence.

Therefore, once we understand the nature of the supreme truth, we establish two corollaries: (a) the supreme truth is the source of all the diversity, and (b) the supreme truth is the goal of all diversity. Thus, diversity is aiming for perfection by the elimination of dualistic, separated, and incomplete nature. Both united and separated natures are semantic because that which is separated is sourced from that which is united and the flaws in it are the result of separation. The separated diversity gets perfection by uniting with what it lacks.

Sūtra 1.2.51

लिङ्गोपदेशश् च तदर्थवत्

liṅgopadeśaś ca tadarthavat

liṅgopadeśa—the teaching of forms, symbols, or representations; ca—also; tadarthavat—just like that meaning.

TRANSLATION

The teaching of forms is also just like that meaning.

COMMENTARY

When people see the forms of God, commonly represented as deities, they imagine that people are worshipping idols when these are material realizations of meaning-forms. The meaning is not destroyed if you break the idol, just like the idea of chair is not destroyed if you break a chair. The chair is only an embodiment of the idea. Since most people cannot understand meaning forms, they are converted into sense-perceivable forms. Ideas such as beauty, justice, power, and wealth are meaning-forms, but we don't see them. To make these forms visible to us, instances of these forms are created as beautiful things, enactments of justice, illustrations of power, and instances of wealth. The supreme truth, according to this sūtra, is also a meaning-form, and He appears like various forms that we can perceive. By associating with these forms, we get an understanding of the nature of beauty, wealth, power, justice, etc. The meaning of 'supreme truth' is that it is the combined form of all the other forms.

In this world, beauty is not always wealthy, and power is not always just. Therefore, the meaning forms are separated in this world, and by that separation, the material world is called 'duality'. But in the supreme truth, these forms are combined, which means that there is beauty but it is not poor; there is power but it is not unjust. The 'supreme truth' is also a form, but that form combines all the individual forms that we perceive separated in the material world.

Even if these forms are separated, whatever is created by that separation still has some form. It may be the form of wealth without beauty, or the form of power without justice. We can call these 'ugly' truths or 'evil' reality, but it is a source of partial truth—in so far as we can see parts of the whole truth. Therefore, this world is also a symbolic representation of meanings, although the meanings we see in this world are partial, as some of the forms are missing. What we call evil or ignorance or suffering is also sourced from the same supreme truth, but it becomes undesirable because of separation of forms. Thus, power without justice, or wealth without beauty, are undesirable and can be called 'evil', but even that evil is a partial symbolic representation of the supreme truth. The purported contradictions between transcendent and mundane realities are therefore not true in an absolute sense, although there is indeed a transcendent or united reality distinct from the mundane or divided reality.

Sūtra 1.2.52

ऊहः

ūhaḥ

ūhaḥ—inferencing and concluding.

TRANSLATION

(The supreme truth) inferences and concludes (the variety of forms).

COMMENTARY

The diversity of this world is produced by the divisions of a single source. In that source, all the forms are combined, just like in the idea of beauty, all the various types of beauties (e.g., a beautiful flower, a beautiful theory, a beautiful mind, etc.) are combined. The diverse forms separate from the original form by a process of self-division. That division separates the original form into many diverse and seemingly contradictory forms—as we noted above, beauty can be poor, and power can be unjust. The diversity manifested from the unity is not just many things, but also many mutually contradictory things due to the presence and absence of various forms. This contradiction was previously noted in the case of the statements of the Vedic texts, and the diversity of the material world. But it was stated that this diversity is unified by the supreme truth. Therefore, after stating that unity reconciles diversity, this sūtra states that unity produces diversity and that production is a logical process of inferencing and concluding from a complex idea (that combines many ideas) to simpler ideas (that are separated). It is easier to understand the ideas of beauty, power, justice, and wealth separately, and harder to understand their combination. Therefore, inferencing is the process of clarifying and expositing a complex nature.

Sūtra 1.2.53

वधिशिब्दाश् च

vidhiśabdāś ca

vidhi—procedures; śabdāt—from the scriptures; ca—also.

TRANSLATION

The procedures from the scriptures are also (manifest from supreme truth).

COMMENTARY

After establishing the transcendental source of the material world, this sūtra states that the Vedas also have a transcendental source. The order is important here. If we say that the Vedas are transcendental, but the world is mundane, we create a discrepancy about how transcendental knowledge arises in the mundane world. If instead, we establish a transcendental source of the material world, then questions about the transcendence of the Vedas become moot. The question only remains: What is that text that combines all the previously noted forms such as beauty, justice, power, wealth, etc.? What is that text that doesn't see a contradiction between these forms? And what is that text that tells us how such seemingly contradictory and disparate ideas can be reconciled?

The Vedas are material in so far as these forms are separated, and they are transcendent in so far as these forms are combined. Factually, in any text, we can only discuss these forms one after another. While discussing the nature of truth, for instance, we are unable to discuss the nature of beauty, and truth and beauty seem disparate and separated. But this is the nature of texts—they are serialized information. The text as a whole, combines all these ideas. Therefore, if we gather these ideas by reading the texts, then we can combine them in our minds and that combination is indeed the vision of the supreme truth.

The Sāñkhya Description of Ego

What we colloquially call the "ego" is a very complex covering of the soul in Vedic philosophy. It comprises four components, namely, (a) the idea that I'm a master called Pradhāna, (b) the desire to exercise mastery in a particular way called Prakṛti, (c) the idea that I possess great qualities called Mahattattva due to which I can exercise mastery, and (d) the pride in the self under the belief of possession of great qualities called Ahaṃkāra. From this Ahaṃkāra manifests the cognitive instrument comprising the intellect, mind, senses, and sensations, the gross body comprising the perceivable elements, and the relationships to other bodies by which social identity is constructed. This post discusses the deconstruction of the colloquial "ego" as described in the Sāñkhya Sūtras. This discussion is illustrative because it shows how the world expands from the (false) idea of mastery into a demonstration of mastery as the subtle and gross existences along with social relationships, but because the proof of demonstration is temporary, therefore, the "ego" is constantly modified until the idea of mastery is given up.

The Social Construction of Identity

Lord Kṛṣṇa describes the ego as *aham mameti* or "I and mine". These two are mutually defined. Who am I? I might say: I am an Indian. In so saying, I have defined myself in relation to a country. Similarly, I might say: I am male. In so saying, I have defined myself in relation to my body. Then, based on this identity, I consider some things to be "mine". For instance, I can say: "This is my body" or "this is my country".

In Western philosophy, this is sometimes called the *social construction* of identity. Postmodernism rests on social construction. It says: Everything that we consider ourselves to be our personal identity is actually based on our relations to the world. In short, our identity is socially constructed. We bear numerous relationships to the world—e.g., a family, employer, nation, race, etc.—and these relationships define "me". Similarly, the things which define me—e.g., family, employer, nation, or race—are defining themselves in relation to me.

If we alter our relationships with the world, then we will change our identity. For example, we can renounce the citizenship of one country and accept the citizenship of another country. By that change, our national identity would be altered. Likewise, I can change my employer, and by that change, I would have altered my professional identity. I can get married or divorced, and by that change, I would have changed my familial identity. I could even change my romantic relationships with other people, and, by that, I would have changed the "socially constructed" identity of gender. In this case, the social construction pertains to the idea that men relate romantically to women (and vice versa). The change to social construction would allow men to relate romantically to other men and women to women.

Three Types of Identity

The trouble with this way of thinking is that whatever we call "identity" has three components—objective, subjective, and intersubjective—so there are objective and subjective identities apart from the socially constructed identity. The body for instance has a gender, which is an objective identity. I might have some personal values, beliefs, thoughts, and sensual preferences that form my subjective identity. Finally, there is also an intersubjective component to the identity, which is defined by my relationship to the race, nation, employer, etc.

The "I" therefore has two aspects—the objective and subjective components of "I". And "mine" is the intersubjective component of the same "I". In an ultimate sense, neither of these three identities stand alone. They must combine to produce a complete identity.

Therefore, "I" is incomplete without "mine", and vice versa. But since they are distinct components, therefore, each component is said to be either dominant or subordinate in forming the identity. For instance, based on a strong subjective identity about a certain gender (e.g., female), one can disregard the objective identity of the body's gender (e.g., male), and the intersubjective identity of relations based on socially construed norms about gender (e.g., that males have romantic relationships to females) and resort to alternative ideas (e.g., a romance between males). In this case, we would say that the subjective identity is dominant, and the objective and intersubjective identities are subordinated.

The Relational Nature of Identity

But there is another sense in which all identity is constructed only out of relationships, which is understood if we see the soul distinct from the body. For instance, we noted that the bodily gender is objective but this is not entirely true; that identity pertains to the body, not the self, and it becomes "my" gender when I identify with the body. Hence, whatever we call an objective identity is not objectively about the soul; it is objectively real but pertains to the body. Therefore, it is not truly "me". Similarly, whatever we call our subjective identity, namely, my values, goals, beliefs, thoughts, and sensations, is actually not truly "mine". They also pertain to a body, which is sometimes called the "subtle body" and sometimes the "gendered body", different from the "gross body" (of hands and legs). All our subjective experiences are caused due to the association of the soul to an objective material reality, although that reality may only be accessible in our experience.

Thus, even our objective and subjective identity is a relational identity—the relation is to the gross and subtle bodies. Then, what we call our intersubjective identity is obviously a relational identity—the relation is established *between* different gross and subtle bodies.

When we realize that even "I" is a relational identity, quite like the "mine", then all ego—which we defined above as "I" and "mine"—becomes a relational identity. This means that we can discard all these identities by stopping the relation to the body and mind. If we give up the attachment to the subjective and objective identity, then the intersubjective identity is also discarded. Conversely, the identity expands from the subjective to the objective to the intersubjective. For instance, my subjective thoughts and perceptions are objectively expressed through the body, which then intersubjectively relate to other bodies. If the subjective identity was destroyed, then all the other identities would also be lost. The "destruction of ego" pertains to the destruction of the deepest identity, namely, of identifying with some beliefs, thoughts, perceptions, etc. because if the subjective identity is destroyed, then the objective and intersubjective identities would be too.

Expansions of the Ego

This idea is succinctly explained in Sāñkhya when the intellect, mind, sensations, senses, and the sense objects are all said to have expanded from the ego. The basic import is that the world is expanding *inside-out,* namely, from the soul's material identity into its expression. This expansion of identity begins in a subjective component (e.g., thoughts and perceptions), then into an objective component (i.e., the gross body), and then into the social worldly relational component of race, nationality, employment, family, property ownership, etc.

Sāñkhya Sūtra further expounds on this idea by stating—"the ego is pride". In short, the subjective, objective, and intersubjective identities are by-products of pride. If we are not proud of our thoughts and perceptions, then we will discard them, and only those thoughts are percetpions that accentuate our pride will be created. If we are not proud of our bodily appearance, then we try to change it (people trying to change their gender is an extreme example of this, but there are other ways in which people try to change their bodily identity by altering their hairstyle, skin tone, clothes, etc.), and those appearances that undermine our pride would be discarded. Finally, if we are not proud of our nationality, race, profession, etc. then we try to change them, and what we accept will be that which makes us proud.

Thus, as the subjective, objective, and relational identities are traced back to the ego, the ego itself is defined as "pride". The subtle and gross bodies, and their relations to other bodies, are hence expanding from the pride. Pride now also becomes the basis on which the ego is said to create our happiness. Basically, when we feel proud, we call it "happiness" and when we don't feel proud, we call it "unhappiness".

Sāñkhya then delves deeper into the origin of the pride and states that it arises from principles of ideality called mahattattva. Basically, to even feel proud, we must think that we are perfect in some sense, and the worldly expression realizes or "proves" that perfection. Then, even this sense of perfection is traced back to some desire to enjoy, which is called prakṛti, because something is ideal only relative to our goals. If our goals are different, then the definition of ideality must be altered. Finally, even this desire to enjoy is traced back to something called the pradhāna or the idea that "I am the boss or master". Thus, material existence begins in the idea of personal mastery, which expands into a desire to exercise a specific type of mastery, which then expands into a certain type of idealism about oneself to attain mastery, which then expands into pride about the self being capable of mastery. This pride is generally called our "self-confidence" in our personal abilities. From this self-confidence progressively expand the subtle body, the gross body, and the relationships to other subtle and gross bodies.

For example, if we want to exercise our mastery through wealth, then prakṛti represents the desire for wealth. Then, mahattattva is the idealism of being capable of earning wealth. Then the ego is the self-confidence in oneself being capable of earning wealth. From this pride emerge beliefs, thoughts, and sensations of wealth, which transform into the gross bodily apparatus, which then leads to relationships.

The Tree of the Root Ego

In simple terms, the world is expanding from our need for mastery to the desire to prove our mastery, to personal qualities that will prove the mastery, to the ego that feels proud of these qualities, to the subjective, objective, and intersubjective expressions of the pride (which is, in turn, the expression of the personal qualities, desires, and ultimately, the need for mastery). Even if the pride is hurt, the idea of mastery, the desire to establish this mastery in a specific way, and the idealism about the self being capable of this mastery are not destroyed; they are temporarily obstructed but they spring again and again into a new reality, until, of course, the need for mastery is completely destroyed.

We can visualize this process as a world springing out much like a tree grows out of a root, such that even if the leaves and branches are cut, the root remains intact and produces new branches and leaves. No matter how many times the leaves and branches are cut, the tree doesn't stop growing unless the root is destroyed. Our desire for proving our mastery may change from the acquisition of wealth to the acquisition of knowledge. Our idealism about the self may change from being capable of earning wealth to capable of acquiring knowledge. Our self-confidence may change from pertaining to wealth to knowledge. And our thoughts, bodies, and relationships may change based on knowledge as opposed to wealth. And yet, despite these superficial changes, the root belief that "I am the master" remains unaffected.

Four Aspects of the Ego

The first four elements of Sāñkhya—namely, pradhāna, prakṛti, mahattattva, and ahaṃkāra—collectively constitute what we colloquially call the "ego". Sāñkhya, of course, uses the term ahaṃkāra to describe the pride in oneself or self-confidence. Since pride is often equated with the "ego" therefore ahaṃkāra is also translated as the "ego", although if we look closely, the idea that I'm a master, that I want to prove my mastery in a certain way, that I'm capable of proving my mastery due to possession of ideal qualities, and the feeling of pride because of the possession of these personal qualities, collectively constitute the "ego". What we colloquially call the "ego" is thus deconstructed into four distinct parts in Sāñkhya, of which "pride" in the self is only a superficial expression of the most primordial idea that "I am a master".

In the Bhagavad-Gita, this four-fold division of the "ego" is summarized into a single entity called the "ego". The text states that there are eight components of the material energy, of which ahaṃkāra is the first. This is a summarized description of the ego in which four components—i.e., pradhāna, prakṛti, mahattattva, and ahaṃkāra are bundled into ahaṃkāra, as they are four facets of the ego.

False Science Created From the Ego

Since intelligence is a by-product of the ego, the implication is that this material intelligence is not suited for knowing the truth. Its sole function is to create theories about the world that prove the mastery of the self, in order to justify our greatness and enhance our pride. Therefore, even when a person is said to be highly intelligent materially, he is still considered foolish, because his intellect is produced from the ego, and it serves the ego. That ego is serving the pride, which is serving the desire for personal mastery. The intellect would be truly great if the idea of mastery was true and real. But if the soul is not truly a master, then all attempts to justify it are ignorance.

The fact is that all intellectual speculation, or what we call modern science, are by-products of the intellect, which is a by-product of the ego, which is trying to prove the false idea of personal mastery of the world. When this intelligence is used for speculation about the world, all theories of nature are produced only to reinstate the idea that we can control and dominate nature, to prove our mastery over nature.

Underlying our scientific endeavors, therefore, is the idea that I will become a master of nature by pursuing scientific progress. Any scientific theory that demonstrates that we have failed to be a master is dismissed as a temporary setback to be soon overcome by a better theory that will reinstate our mastery. Even when a scientific theory conclusively demonstrates that we have failed irrevocably and that we cannot perfectly control and dominate nature by our will, some "interpretation" of the theory is created to prove that we are still masters.

For instance, when it became clear that the scientific method cannot reveal the nature of reality, due to irrevocable failures of empiricism and rationalism, then Pragmatism was created as the "epistemology" of science to claim that even if we cannot know nature, that failure isn't so bad if we produce working technology. If the technology works, it doesn't matter if we know the truth, because science is a tentative "working model". In short, even if our "knowledge" is not the truth, it is not so bad if we can blind the public to our failure via technology. This is the nature of the ego—it rationalizes a failure as the gate to a new heaven, to perpetuate the sense of false grandeur.

False Religion Created from Ego

Similarly, many false religions are produced from the ego as means to control others. For example, a religious leader may sometimes describe himself as the embodiment of God on Earth. Many political leaders often portray themselves as God's gift to mankind. These leaders use religion as a tool to propagate their own power and try to demonstrate their own supremacy rather than God's supremacy.

In another form, many people treat transcendence as another type of egoistic achievement. They want to transcend the world by their own effort, knowledge, yoga practice, and so on, and don't want to recognize the supremacy of God. They present themselves as "spiritual" rather than "religious" because in their "religion" the self is supreme and the supremacy of God thereby need not be recognized.

In yet another form, many "gurus" who accept God's supremacy may still want to use religion to create a second-level mastery by accumulating power, wealth, and followers. That situation is not different from an ordinary person trying to prove their mastery through the acquisition of worldly wealth and power. The outward expression of the ego in terms of dress, words, and relationships may seem different. But the root is the same. Such a person is not truly a master nor is he a guru. He is still a servant of the same egoistic principle.

Then, in another form, religion is tied to materialistic ideas of race, nationality, the pursuit of wealth, the exercise of global power, etc. All these pursuits are justified as the rewards furnished by God to His followers and pursuits of power and prestige are justified as religion.

These false, pretentious, and imaginary religions do not lead one to transcendence; they keep the soul bound because they are rooted in the ego principle which is the cause of material existence. Since the ego can produce literally infinite variety, it can produce both overt and covert materialistic identities. The overt materialistic identity appears in the form of blatant pursuit of wealth, power, control, and followers. But the covert materialistic identity can appear in the pursuit of mystical powers, greed for a powerful position in a religious organization, and philosophical justifications of the self being the supreme. The latter are not fundamentally better than the former.

Therefore, materialistic religions are as much a product of the ego as scientific materialism; both products have a singular aim to prove that the self is the master. They rationalize all their failures as temporary setbacks and take solace in their limited successes. They can appear to be vastly different but they are produced from the same desire to justify, rationalize, and demonstrate one's mastery of the world.

Understanding Satkāryavāda: Correlation vs. Causation

The Doctrine of Satkāryavāda

If you put your hand in the fire, it will be burnt. Science will say: Fire is energy; when you bring your hand in contact with fire, then energy is transferred to your hand, and that causes the burn. Likewise, if you jump off a cliff, you will die. Science will say: The body on top of the cliff has gravitational potential energy; when you jump off the cliff, that potential energy is converted into kinetic energy, and since the body cannot tolerate so much kinetic energy, therefore, you will die. Sounds perfectly reasonable?

Maybe not. The Śrīmad Bhagavatam describes the story of Prahalāda, who sat in a fire along with his sister Holika, upon the instruction of their father Hiraṇyakaśīpu. Holika had the mystic power of not being burnt by fire, and she thought that she would be saved while Prahalāda would be burnt. But the reverse happened. The sister got burnt while Prahalāda was unaffected by the fire. When Prahalāda was thrown from mountain tops upon the instruction of his father Hiraṇyakaśīpu, he was never hurt.

Miracle and magic? Maybe not. What we think of as *causation* in science—e.g., that putting your hand in fire will burn the hand—is a *correlation*, not a *causation*. Namely, there is the event of a fire, and then there is the event of burning, and most of the time these two occur together. Since they mostly occur together, therefore, we can say that they are correlated. However, they do not occur always, so there is no causal necessity between fire and burning. Since it happens most of the time, therefore, we think there is a law of nature. When that law isn't upheld then we think it must be magic and a miracle.

To understand the distinction between correlation and causation, we have to envision an inverted tree in which causes propagate from the root to the trunks to the branches to the twigs to the leaves. This is called Satkāryavāda. In this doctrine, the effect emerges out of a cause, just like a trunk grows out of a root, a branch grows out of a trunk, a twig grows out of a branch, and a leaf grows out of the twig.

Effect Hidden Inside the Cause

Some of you might have heard of Matryoshka dolls. There is a doll inside a doll, inside a doll. You open one doll, and you see another doll inside it. Then you open that second doll, and you see the third doll inside that. Nature is just like these Matryoshka dolls, and nature's manifestations are like opening one doll after another, such that each opening of the doll reveals a new doll. Therefore, wood is one doll, and fire is another doll inside that wood doll. And the manifestation of fire from wood involves opening the outer doll to reveal the inner doll. The fire revealed from the wood is not energy transferred from outside the wood. That fire was always hidden inside the bigger doll; it just wasn't visible to us.

In the same way, Satkāryavāda says that fire was *latent* in the wood, and it has been *manifest* from the wood subsequently. The wood is just like a twig and the fire is like a leaf growing on that twig. The leaf comes out of the twig, and the fire comes out of the wood, although it was previously latent.

The Example of Fire Manifestation

In the Vedic system, the fire in the wood was called *araṇi*. While performing a yajñá, the fire wasn't lighted by using another fire; rather, the fire was manifest out of wood, by chanting mantras. Of course, nobody knows how to do that today, so we use a matchbox. But that fire which is lighted using a secondary source of fire carries the properties of the secondary source, so it is not considered suitable for yajñá.

The light particles "emitted" by a matchbox are not just packets of energy; they carry information about their source. Due to carrying source information, there is a difference between sitting in sunlight and under tube light. The light particle carries source information and embeds it in the destination, such that the destination gets the property of the source. So, if you sit in the sunlight, then you get the property of effulgence like the sun. But if you sit in a tube light, then you get the property of a tube light. If a matchbox is used to light the *araṇi* then it carries the properties of the matchbox. That kind of fire is not considered suitable for a yajñá. Similarly, all kinds of wood are not considered suitable for yajñá. A specific kind of wood, triggered by certain kinds of mantras produces a specific kind of fire, which is considered suitable for yajñá.

Back to the main point about fire being latent in wood, from where it can be manifest. There are many ways in which we can manifest the fire: (a) by chanting mantras, (b) rubbing pieces of wood together, (c) by using a secondary source of fire, etc. The fire produced by rubbing wood or a secondary source of fire falls into the category that modern science can explain: Basically, energy is seemingly transferred from one place to another. But the fire produced by a mantra cannot be explained in this way, because the energy was latent and it has been manifested without transferring energy. Science also cannot explain why something would not light up when subjected to fire, hence the puzzlement of Prahalāda story.

Horizontal and Vertical Causation

The scientific model of causality can be contrasted to the Vedic model in the inverted tree model. The scientific model says that one fire causes another fire, which is like saying that one leaf produced another leaf. In science, fire in the match lights up the wood, through a *horizontal* transfer of energy from leaf to leaf. But in the Vedic model, there is no horizontal path from one leaf to another leaf; all leaves are connected to each other through branches, trunks, and the root. Therefore, causation is always *vertical*: From the root to the trunk to the branch to the leaf. You can again think of two Matryoshka doll sets. You open the outer doll in one set, and the outer doll in another set is opened simultaneously.

This simultaneity in the opening of two doll sets gives the impression that opening one doll is the *cause* of the opening of another doll. But that is not true; there are two separate doll sets that are being opened individually, but there is a correlation between the opening of the two doll sets. That is, *generally,* if you open one doll, the other doll opens as well. That correlation is not causation, as each doll is controlled separately. Science converts this correlation into causation, but Vedic philosophy does not. It says: Each doll is separately controlled, and the effect comes out from *within* the cause.

Correlation is Not Causation

In summary, just because two events occur simultaneously or one after another doesn't mean that one is the cause of another. It doesn't matter how many times you can repeat that experiment and confirm the recurrence. All these recurrences of events are simply correlations between two occurrences. They do not establish causality. In modern terminology, correlation of events is not event causation.

In Satkāryavāda, the real *causation* is from the root to the trunk to the branch to the leaf. However, because many such leaves may be produced as effects simultaneously, therefore, there is also a *correlation* between leaf-to-leaf. Everything that modern science does is based on this correlation. It says: If you light a match, then you can burn the wood. Since causation has to be *necessary* and *sufficient,* therefore, one must also say that every time a match is lighted, the wood must also burn (this is called necessity) and nothing other than the match is required to light the wood (this is called sufficiency). But in Satkāryavāda, this leaf-to-leaf correlation is not causation; it is just the *appearance* of causality if we don't know that the true causation is coming out from a deeper reality of root, trunk, branch.

When we light a match to burn wood, the light doesn't move from match to wood. This idea of causation is an illusion. Rather, the causality moves upward from the leaf to the branch. This upward movement of the cause involves deeper realities like the senses, mind, intellect, ego, etc. As it moves upward, there are universal administrators for unique types of leaves. For instance, to manifest fire from the wood, there is an administrator called Agni. He approves our desire to light the wood using the match. Then, by the will of Agni, the cause moves downward, and fire is manifest from wood.

Two things are happening simultaneously—(a) a fire is lighted in the match, and (b) a fire is lit in the wood. But their simultaneous occurrence is merely a *correlation*. The real cause is Agni who approves the transfer of causality from the match to the wood. Thereby, causation moves up from leaf to branch and then moves downward from the branch to another leaf. This upward and downward movement of the cause is real *causation*, while the match lighting the wood is just *correlation*. We can imagine this process as one of request and approval; our desire to do something is a request that moves upward and gets approved by an administrator. Then it moves downward and is executed.

Understanding Prahalāda's Story Scientifically

Therefore, when Prahalāda sits on the fire, Holika's intention to burn Prahalāda moved upward, but Agni rejected that request. Instead, Agni sent down another instruction to Holika's body, that manifested fire from Holika's body. Effectively, Holika got self-immolated, as fire manifested from her body, just like fire manifests from wood. Lord Shiva's wife (Sati) also self-immolated Herself when Her husband was insulted by Her father Daksha. This self-immolation by manifesting fire within the body to burn the body is considered a legitimate form of suicide in the Vedic system. Of course, fools, later on, started burning widow brides and this tradition also erroneously came to be known as "Sati" after Lord Shiva's wife. But there is a big difference between burning a bride—which is murder—and self-immolation, which is suicide.

To the naïve vision, it seems that the burning wood caused the burning of Holika. But the simultaneous presence of fire in the wood and in Holika's body are mere correlations between two separate events. The true cause of burning is the deeper cause that manifests a superficial phenomenon. This can be based on a mystic power, the chanting of mantras, or even the direction of the demigods.

Satkāryavāda Used in Weaponry

The process of manifesting fire in something to burn it was formerly employed in weapons. For example, there is an Agni mantra that can be chanted to request Agni to burn something, and by Agni's direction, the requested thing can be automatically lit up in flames. Such weapons were in use in the Mahabharata war, and the use of these weapons illustrates this process quite well. A warrior chants a mantra and shoots an arrow. When the arrow hits the target, the target is lit up in flames. In the superficial vision, we might wonder: How can the arrow light up a target? And the answer is: It is not the arrow that lights up the target; that arrow is simply selecting a destination to be lit up, and Agni—the demigod—manifests the fire hidden in the thing and causes it to self-immolate.

The shooting of the arrow and the lighting of the target are just mutually correlated; the cause of burning the target is the demigod Agni. Such weapons were generally gifted to the warriors by demigods themselves, by informing them of the mantras. For instance, in the Mahabharata, there is a detailed description of how Arjuna received these weapons from the demigods. That gift involves a mantra to be kept secret and privileged. We can imagine how much destruction would be caused today if ordinary people got such weapons.

Just as Agni can approve requests to light up things, similarly, he can also deny requests. The fire of the wood on which Prahalāda was sitting did not burn him, because the request to burn him can be denied by Agni. Since these requests can be denied, therefore, all laws of science that are based on observed correlations are false; they are not actually necessary, but they appear to work mostly because the request is approved based on our karma. If karma is absent, then, we will not get access to burn something, or even if we get access, our attempts to burn it will fail in some way. We would call that "bad luck". But it is not luck. There is a science of request, approval, and denial, by which an arrow can cause fire, a fire may manifest automatically without an external cause, and the presence of fire may not burn the thing.

When science creates laws of necessity and sufficiency based on correlations, then all these phenomena become aberrations. We either think of them as magic or utterly false (mostly the latter). Most people today for instance think that weapons of fire were imaginary because they are always thinking of horizontal rather than vertical causation. Likewise, they think that nature is working according to mathematical laws rather than the intervention of demigods because these mathematical laws seem to work most times.

How God Intervenes in the World

When a devotee surrenders to Krishna, then Krishna becomes the approver or denier of everything. It doesn't matter if the devotee is put into the fire, or thrown from mountains. The Lord will deny all requests and that is His protection. To the naïve vision, it would seem that the mountains have become soft as cushions and the fire has become pleasing like a mild breeze. And so, someone can say: This must be magic and miracle. But it is not magic or miracle; it is completely scientific because the cause doesn't move horizontally; it moves vertically.

So, anybody who wants to hurt the devotee, a request has to go up, has to be approved, and then it can move down to manifest an effect. For the devotee, the Lord denies all such requests. Or, even if He allows them, there is an ulterior reason. For example, sometimes the Lord wants to glorify His devotees in this world; He does so by putting them through difficulties whereby they can show their immense graciousness. When ordinary people see that graciousness, then they accept the devotee as a perfect personality. If the Lord had protected the devotee, then he would never have been glorified in this way. So, the ulterior motives can be to glorify the devotees. It doesn't matter how we think of these things from our vantage point. The devotee of the Lord always understands the true intentions of the Lord and acts accordingly.

If we serve a pure devotee, then the Lord is pleased to approve the request to serve His devotee, and by serving the pure devotee, we are automatically pleasing the Lord. The Lord's pleasure is that He is thrilled and delighted to receive the requests to serve His devotees, and He volunteers to enable their execution. There is hence no difference between serving the Lord's devotee and pleasing the Lord. The Lord is automatically being pleased when the devotee is being served; this too is a scientific principle.

Thus, God's intervention in the world doesn't require an exemption from science. That is because all the laws that modern science claims to discover are merely correlations, not causation. True causation is that we have free will, and God has free will. We propose and God disposes; He approves or disapproves our request. In the material world, our requests are approved by demigods based on our karma. If we have the requisite karma, then the demigods generally approve our requests; if we don't, then those requests are denied. In short, our requests are going up to the demigods and approved or denied by them. This is the hierarchical process of material causation. But if we become devotees of Krishna, then the requests always go to Krishna, and He may approve them. In simple words, material life means requests go up to demigods for approval, and spiritual life means requests go to Krishna for approval. No cause is moving horizontally; all causes are vertical.

Modern scientific atheism is built upon the idea that causes propagate horizontally—from leaf to leaf. So, scientists think that there is no higher authority, no demigod, and ultimately there is no God; the laws of science are doing everything. They don't realize that these laws are merely correlations, not causation. Scientists tabulate correlations (i.e., event X is followed by event Y) and then find a formula that fits that table of correlations. That formula is now called the law of nature. Since these formulas work most of the time, therefore, science claims there is no God. However, true causation appears when these laws stop working, or exceptions to these laws are found. That's when we can revisit the nature of causation and understand that true causality is vertical, not horizontal.

God's Involvement in a Devotee's Life

Everything is moving by the will of Krishna. Some of these movements are because lower-level administrators such as Agni have been authorized to approve or deny requests; that authorization delegates Krishna's will to the demigods. However, this delegation of authority and power also means that Krishna is not directly involved in the delivery of material results, because He is delegating.

Krishna gets directly involved in delivering the results when one becomes a devotee of Krishna. For example, Krishna says in the Bhagavad-Gita 9.22, yoga-kṣhemaṁ vahāmyaham. The term yoga-kṣhemaṁ means the "well-being of yoga", the term vahāmi means carrying, and the term aham means "I" in the first person. So, yoga-kṣhemaṁ vahāmyaham means "I personally carry the burden of the well-being of yoga". However, this happens only when the first part of the verse is also true, namely, "There are those who always think of Me and engage in exclusive devotion to Me. To them, whose minds are always absorbed in Me" followed by "I personally carry the burden of the well-being of yoga".

Śrila Prabhupāda translates yoga-kṣhemaṁ vahāmyaham as "I provide what they (the devotees) lack and preserve what they have". This is his heartfelt realization that Krishna provides everything whenever it is needed. In all of these translations, the main point is that Krishna is personally involved in providing what we lack and preserving what we have, or carrying the burden of the wellness of our yoga practice—provided we are always thinking of Krishna and devoted to Him.

True Science Leads to Devotion

So, devotion to Krishna is also a scientific process, and Krishna becomes personally involved in protecting the devotee if the devotee is always thinking of Krishna. For those who are not thinking of Krishna, the process of approval and denial is delegated to demigods. In the Vedic system, even these non-devotees knew that there is a process of higher approval for everything. But in the modern atheistic system of science, there are no higher authorities, no approval, just impersonal mathematical laws that are concocted by studying correlations, and falsely claimed to be causation.

This atheistic mentality is very painful for the devotees to listen to, so they get angry at the atheists. But that is not because the devotees fear or hate the atheists; it is because they are in love with Krishna. Out of love for Krishna, they cannot listen to the Lord being belittled or disparaged; so, they become angry. The impersonalists have no such love or concern; so, they remain very peaceful and nonchalant. That peace and nonchalance can be compared to the inactivity of a fool who doesn't know the truth.

The devotees can see how Krishna is personally carrying them through this world, always protecting them, guiding them, inspiring them, and yet, never forcing anyone's free will to love or reject Him. Where can we find such a Lord who is all-powerful, and yet, so loving toward His devotees? Therefore, one of the names of the Lord is Bhakta-Vatsala Hari. The word "vatsa" means a child, and "vatsal" means the love of the parent for the child. The Lord protects the devotees like a lioness protects her cub. Sometimes it appears that the lioness is carrying the cub in her vice-like teeth, but that is only mundane vision; the cub feels no pain. In the same way, it sometimes appears that the devotees are put into difficulties, but that is just mundane vision; the devotees feel no pain.

Therefore, the conclusion of Bhagavad-Gita is that one must simply surrender to Krishna. Since most people will not do that, therefore, there is a philosophy of Satkāryavāda to explain the vertical model of causation. Since most people cannot understand what Satkāryavāda is, therefore, we endeavor to explain it through modern jargon such as causation and correlation, necessity and sufficiency, and imperfect illustrations like Matryoshka dolls, elucidating a general principle that applies as much to lighting the *araṇi* as to weapons of fire.

As we try to explain more and more, we seem to keep going farther and farther from the conclusion of surrender to Krishna. But the hope is that if we can wash the materialistic dirt of the false idea of causation, then we can understand hierarchical causation. By that, we can see how Krishna controls everything by His will. Thereafter, we can surrender to Krishna and shed tears of love and gratitude, and this complicated jargon will become inconsequential.

Objections Against My Vedānta Sūtra Commentary

There are occasional rumblings against my Vedānta Sūtra commentary entitled Conceiving the Inconceivable: A Scientific Commentary on Vedānta Sūtras. I understand that many people come to religion with a sense of finality: Worldly knowledge changes, but spiritual knowledge is eternal. In their view, a new commentary breaks that finality. They may view the commentary as breaking the tradition. They question my intentions, attitudes, or qualifications to comment. It is painful to listen to personal attacks. In the introduction to the commentary, I have laid out the reasons why Vedānta seems inconceivable: Vedic philosophy is based on qualities but Vedānta interpretations have been trying to interpret it in terms of quantities. Quality thinking requires non-binary logic, hierarchy instead of linearity, oneness and difference rather than oneness or difference. Quantity thinking is instead based on binary logic, oneness (Brahman) or difference (māyā), transcendence (by oneness) vs. bondage (by difference). It was introduced into Vedānta by Shankaracharya, and it has held Vedānta hostage for over a thousand years. Successive Acharyas have tried to solve the problems resulting from quantity thinking without fully rejecting it. The Achintya Bhedābheda doctrine says that we cannot resolve this problem because all these are logically contradictory ideas. My commentary says that we can resolve them if we change our thinking from quantities to qualities.

But many people overlook all these issues either because they are not interested in Vedic philosophy or because they are more attached to finality rather than understanding how these seeming contradictions can be reconciled. This post lays out these problems for those who might not have read the commentary and answers them using the why-what-how-who structure that addresses the most important questions first and the least important ones last. Responses to personal attacks are the final section.

Why

Prabhupāda's Instructions

All commentaries on Vedānta have been written upon the commands of spiritual authority, after a careful study of their teachings. My commentary is no different. Instructions for writing a "scientific commentary" on Vedanta were given by Śrila Prabhupāda, and this is not a secret either. Many people are aware of such instructions. I have personally heard recorded conversations with Śrila Prabhupāda that were dedicated specifically to the writing of such a commentary. These instructions were imparted to H.H. Bhaktisvarūpa Dāmodar Swāmi, as the director of Bhaktivedānta Institute. I have also excerpted a part of that discussion at the beginning of my commentary.

Prabhupāda was certainly aware of the Gaudīya Vaishnava commentary on Vedānta Sūtra authored by Baladeva Vidyābhushan, referring to it many times in books and lectures. And yet, he asked not for an English translation of his commentary, but for a new commentary. Why he did so, has never been explicit. Are there problems in the Baladeva Vidyābhushan commentary? Will the new commentary supersede it? In what ways will the new commentary differ from the previous one? We don't know the answer to these questions, because nobody asked Prabhupāda these questions. So many other questions about budgets and infrastructure were asked and answered, but not these.

It is understandable if people are confused about such questions, so in the following sections, I will try to explain how we can understand them. These are not substitutes for Prabhupāda's instructions, but they are important to understand how they must be executed. The general principle of understanding is to grasp the "context" in which they were made. That context is all the reasons that Prabhupāda wanted a scientific institute. So, they are in a sense, tied to his idea of "science" which is quite different from what most people currently think science is, and how we should approach it.

Prabhupāda's Vision for Science

Prabhupāda had a very different view of science than what prevails today.

Modern science arose in Europe due to the Protestant Reformation and Enlightenment, which tried to *separate* the questions of matter from the questions of soul and God. The Cartesian mind-body dualism separated the soul from matter. Deism separated God from the material world. The Protestant Reformation laid down principles of separation of individuals whereby the collective contracts of the Jews in Israel or those of the Catholic Church on behalf of humanity were replaced by separate personal contracts with God. These ideas were then applied to the material world, conceiving it as a set of separated particles, governed by some laws of push and pull.

I have earlier discussed the religious origins of modern science in other places (see the articles The Self As the Basis of Science and Mechanistic Theories and Social Science), and we can summarize those discussions succinctly. The genesis of modern science lies in the *separation* of things: (a) all souls are separate from each other, (b) God is separate from the material world, (c) the material world is many separate objects. All these separate things are tied through contracts and laws. All these laws and contracts are negotiable and hence not eternal. Thereby, there is no *truth*. The laws of nature, morality, or religion are not *truths*. They are negotiable contracts, they have been negotiated in a particular way right now, and they are prone to change.

Contrast this idea of reality with that in Vedic philosophy, where the principle is: Neither totally separate nor totally identical. This is called Bhedābheda. We cannot study the world as independent particles, because matter has some oneness apart from the separation. We cannot separate matter from God because matter is an energy of God, that originally rested within Him, and presently operates under His will. We cannot have a contractual society of independent individuals competing for survival, because individuals are not totally separate from society or other individuals. We cannot have a contractual religion because contracts require independence and the soul is never independent of God. The laws of nature are not universal; different places in the universe can have different laws. These laws can evolve with time and different laws can apply in different contexts and situations. However, that is not the negotiability of the laws; it is the contextuality of the law.

We can contrast modern science to the thinking in Vedic philosophy, by a simple dichotomy—separated vs. integrated. Integration entails that we cannot separate science from religion, soul from God, soul from matter, matter from God, individual from other individuals, etc. Thereby, everything in Vedic science changes due to a single idea: separated vs. integrated.

This simple idea of integration can become very hard for people conditioned to think about "science" and "religion" based on separations created by the Protestant Reformation and Enlightenment. But Prabhupāda was not influenced by these Western ideas. For him, Vedic scriptures are not "religion"; they are also science. Similarly, "science" doesn't mean physics, chemistry, biology, mathematics, etc. It rather means a deeper understanding of Vedic philosophy—i.e., how the soul, God, and matter—are simultaneously one and different. This fact is also evident even from a casual look at Vedic scriptures. For example, Lord Krishna speaks about the material nature in the Bhagavad-Gita, sometimes calling it divine, then calling it inferior energy, that operates like a machine under God's control, divided into eight parts. Similarly, the Śrīmad Bhagavatam delves into the nature of matter (called Sāñkhya) and the cosmic structure. We cannot separate science from religion in the way that Protestant Reformation and Enlightenment conceived it. Rather, even the understanding of matter comes from the same book that defines religion.

Prabhupāda's view of science can be gleaned from the fact that he envisioned a program of academics in which the Bachelor's degree in science will teach Bhagavad-Gita, the Master's degree in science will teach Śrīmad Bhagavatam, and the Ph.D. degree in science will teach Chaitanya Charitamrita. What most people consider "religion" was "science" for Prabhupāda because the science-religion dichotomy is an invention of Western Enlightenment and Protestant Reformation, and it should not be carried into the Vedic system.

Prabhupāda spoke about the "science of Krishna consciousness" and instructed his disciples to "write books to show that God is a person". His idea of science was the "science of the soul". Everything, including God, is a soul because a soul simply means a person. Evolution meant how the soul goes from one conscious experience to another. Cosmology meant the collection of all possible conscious experiences. These were the two urgent projects that Prabhupāda had for Bhaktivedānta Institute. Explain the universe as the collection of many kinds of experiences. And explain how the soul moves from one experience to another, which is evolution and transmigration.

How Enlightenment Thinking Conditions Us

In the Vedic system, science and religion are distinct as theory and practice, not as the study of matter vs. God and soul. Science in the Vedic system does not mean experiments; that experimentation is a religious practice by which we realize the nature of the truth. Likewise, religion can be practiced without fully knowing the science. Hence, one can chant the names of God, or worship the deity, without fully understanding the philosophy of soul and God. This is the essence of the science-religion distinction in the Vedic sense; it doesn't mean matter vs. soul and God. It means theory vs. practice. But almost everyone today thinks that science means the study of matter while religion means the study of the soul and God. This is due to centuries of conditioning created by Western thinking.

If we understand science as a rigorous, detailed, and extensive philosophical analysis of the Vedic scriptures, then Vedānta is science. However, if we think that science means the study of matter, then Vedānta is religion. I doubt that people can shake off their Western conditioning on science and religion easily. Hence, it can be hard for them to think that Bhagavad-Gita or Śrīmad Bhagavatam is science. For them, they are religion. But for Prabhupāda, a scientist is one who deeply understands these books, and religionists are those who may read a few things and primarily focus on the practice, although not deeply understand these books.

Under this view, Vedānta is also science. But that is not unique to Vedānta. Even advanced topics about the love of God are in the purview of science. Science is just that aspirational state of deep understanding of the Vedic texts, while religion is the common state of practicing the processes of spiritual upliftment without a complete understanding of the texts.

The Importance of Science for Prabhupāda

Enlightenment thinking has conditioned people to reject anything that is not based on reason and observation. If we cannot explain the nature of the soul and God based on reason and observation, then it will be called "faith". Similarly, anything that is based on "faith" would also be rejected as being inferior to knowledge that is based on reason and observation.

Reasoning and observation, however, are not the only basis of modern thinking; there is always an *ideology* behind reasoning, which constitutes the axioms of reasoning, which are used to interpret observations. That ideology of modern thinking is the doctrine of *separation* between souls, God, and material objects. If we change the ideology, then we change the axioms used in reasoning and the interpretation of all observations. If our reasoning is based on the ideology of separation, then we will see the world as independent particles and use these ideas to *interpret* the observed data. However, if our thinking is based upon the ideology of "oneness and difference" then we will use that alternative lens to interpret the *same* data.

This data can be fossil records of evolution, the movements of rockets, airplanes, cars, etc., the observations of the cosmos, the observation of the atoms, chemical reactions, biological phenotypes, the rise and fall of economics, the dynamics of organizations in a society, the psychological phenomena, etc. If separation is a false idea, then all modern scientific interpretations will fail to correctly account for the data. Conversely, "oneness and difference" will correctly explain all the data. In fact, because separation is also not entirely false in oneness and difference thinking, therefore, science will always be *partially* successful in accounting for empirical data—to the extent that the separation idea is true—but fail in many ways because that separation is not the only truth; we have to also think of the integration in reality.

The Bhedābheda doctrine can thus be established by the fact that it *better explains the data*. Then we cannot say that Vedic philosophy is irrational or unempirical. We can also refute all other religions based on the core idea of separation by the fact that they are not working for the data of this world.

This is an *Archimedes Lever* in which you use the *data* of science to refute scientific theories and other religions. Prabhupāda quoted a Bengali proverb to illustrate this idea: "using your mortar and pestle, I am going to break your teeth". The "teeth" in question refer to the false prestige associated with science and other religions. He also said that this presentation will "enhance the prestige of ISKCON". Thereby, we get the second use of science, which is to undermine other ideologies. It is slightly different in focus from studying and understanding Vedic texts deeply, but they are not independent.

In short, now we get two ideas: (a) study Vedic scriptures deeply because that study is science, and (b) apply that study to interpret the data of science to refute its theories and other religions. The former idea is traditional, and the latter idea arises in the context that Vedic religion is going global. Since it is no longer confined to the Indian subcontinent, how do you handle the attacks from other ideologies? How do you show that the Vedic system is superior, rational, empirical, and theologically better? The answer is: We are more *scientific*, and we can prove that by applying our ideas to worldly data.

Issues of Religious Modernization

The Gaudīya tradition has been extremely innovative since the time of Bhaktivinode Thakur. He is the first one to start writing books in English. To understand its significance, we have to note the fact that the Gaudīya tradition never translated books into Arabic or Urdu, although India was under Islamic rule when the

Gaudīya tradition started. While the Vedic culture prohibited people from traveling to other lands and mixing with people from them, Bhaktivinode Thakur envisioned a worldwide community of devotees. Then, Bhaktisiddhānta Saraswati instituted "preaching" as a spiritual activity, which was never the case in the Vedic system; preaching was at that time the sole prerogative of Christianity. While Bengali intellectuals were fighting against the "caste system", Bhaktisiddhānta Saraswati was advocating Varṇāśrama. They went against the Vedic tradition and the Indian culture of the time.

Similarly, Prabhupāda added the mission of scientific presentation of Krishna consciousness. He could not fulfill the mission in his lifetime in the same way that Bhaktivinode Thakur could not establish a worldwide mission dedicated to preaching the mission of Lord Chaitanya in his lifetime. The reason we know of such a mission today is that Prabhupāda fulfilled it subsequently.

The mission of a scientific presentation of Krishna consciousness is Prabhupāda's modernization of the Gaudīya tradition. We cannot find any precedent of a scientific presentation of religion before him. But that is no different than the fact that we cannot find books written in English before Bhaktivinode Thakur. Or the establishment of preaching missions before Bhaktisiddhānta Saraswati. The mission of scientific presentation of religion is presently unfulfilled in the same sense that Bhaktivinode Thakur's vision of a worldwide league of devotees was unfulfilled for a very long time, or Bhaktisiddhānta Sarasvati's vision of Varṇāśrama is unfulfilled today. The Acharyas lay down a vision and instruction, asking it to be executed. That vision is perfect, but it has to be realized through effort and dedication.

The essence of that vision is that the Gaudīya tradition will lead all other traditions in an intellectual revolution. This is the equivalent of Enlightenment in the West in terms of intellectual reformation in natural sciences, social sciences, mind sciences, logical sciences, life sciences, and philosophy. Any difficulty one has in understanding that vision can be resolved by casting this in terms of how Enlightenment transformed Europe and then the whole world through ideological changes making European thinking global.

This is an audacious vision, but no more audacious than Bhaktivinode Thakur dreaming of a worldwide league of devotees, while sitting in a small house, under British rule. It is also no more audacious than Prabhupāda calling his small band of hippies the "International Society for Krishna Consciousness". It seems audacious to those who might not think Prabhupāda's words true.

This modernization of religion is due to the globalization of an ideology that was previously confined to the Indian subcontinent. It is needed because the modern world gives so much importance to the ideas of modern science. When you take a new way of thinking to people unfamiliar with it, then you have to adapt it to suit the manner in which they can accept it.

The Global Decline of Religion

It is well known that religion is declining everywhere. Whatever remains of religiosity is mostly blind faith fanatic followers, who are increasingly uneducated and violent. This decline is a direct consequence of the numerous false ideas in Abrahamic religions, which have been forced upon people through violence, conquest, intimidation, and coercion. The world is no longer prepared for false ideas being foisted upon them through brute force. So, if religion is equated to "faith" and "belief", then it will automatically be rejected by almost all educated people. The rapid rise of atheism in the West is due to the irrationality of religions and their use of violence.

Atheism impacts complex religions far more than simpler religions. The Vedic religion is more complex because it includes karma and reincarnation, deity worship, mantra chanting, rituals, incarnations, more heavens and hells, more demigods and demons, many universes, many spiritual planets, masculine and feminine forms of God, and many forms of God, all of which are discussed to varying levels of detail in different texts, in response to different concerns. In contrast, Abrahamic religions are very simple, as they remove all of the above things from religion, and we are left with one universe in which one earth has human life, one God, one heaven, and one scripture. Impersonalism and Buddhism are even simpler—as they even remove the soul and God from religion—and describe the world as being unreal in some sense.

When atheism rises in society, then complex religions are impacted far more than simpler religions. People can then only accept simpler religions, which is why impersonalism and voidism are rising in the West because they are *simpler* compared to the Abrahamic religions. When the global trend is toward this simplification, then how do you make a more complex religion more popular? Every new idea you add to religion will contribute to additional complexity, and make it harder for people to accept it. The answer is: You have to do exponentially more philosophy and science to explain the complexity.

If we cannot do that, then the complex religion will decline rapidly even in places where it has prospered formerly. India is a good example of this problem as many "scientifically educated" people in India have begun to question Indian traditions, including temples and deities. They are also moving rapidly toward a simpler religion based on impersonalism. One common political issue arising from this trend is: Our temples have thousands of tons of gold and jewelry. Why can't we sell all of that and feed the poor? If we cannot explain how the deity is God, and His temple is His home, then one of two things will happen: (a) there will be a violent group of fanatics who will protect temples and alienate everyone else, (b) the educated people will grow increasingly distrustful of religion and equate it to fanatic blind faith.

The same issue exists when the Vedic system spreads to other parts of the world, where it encounters other religions with simpler ideologies in which the people are growing tired even of the current complexity. If we cannot make this far more complicated religion accessible to people through extensive philosophy and science, then most people will go toward atheism, and some people will go toward a far simpler religion—e.g., impersonalism or voidism. The counter to materialism and atheism will therefore be impersonalism and voidism, and it will be much harder to speak of a complicated religion.

This is the third sense in which Prabhupāda envisioned the use of science—not merely as a deeper study of the Vedic texts, and not just as a superior science and better religion—but also as a tool to arrest the spread of impersonalism and voidism. Now, science has another significance: "Use science to prove that God is a person". Atheism replaces God's deities with technology idols. Impersonalism and voidism try to break down all idols. But neither are correct positions. We have to idolize the Lord instead of idolizing technology or rejecting all idolatry. The world is meaningful to the extent that it embodies the qualities of God. Hence, there are greater and lesser meaningful things in this world. If we cannot show why some idols are more meaningful, then atheism will replace them with technology idols while impersonalism and voidism will continue trying to break down all forms of idolatry.

What

The Problem of Inconceivability

Once we grasp the role of science in the modernization of religion, then we have to contend with the key issue: Bhedābheda is inconceivable. We can go to a philosopher, scientist, modernist, impersonalist, or voidist and proclaim: We know the nature of the truth, and it is that everything is simultaneously one and different from all the other things but I cannot explain that to you rationally because it is inconceivable. What do you think is going to happen? Will the opponent give you the benefit of the doubt: Maybe he analyzed everything perfectly and then concluded that reality is indeed inconceivable? Or will he say: He most likely made no effort before making such a claim?

We can make the Achintya claim among Vedānta stalwarts because they are aware of the succession of problems that arise from each position. Thereby, we can rule out the positions of total ignorance or lack of attempts. But we cannot make the claim among those unfamiliar with the Vedic system. In fact, in a world where everyone asserts the certainty of their claims with a greater force based on observation and reason, the claim of inconceivability would be easily rejected as being *more* suspect than claims of partial truth.

The basic issue is that inconceivability is a non-starter for any kind of science. Bhedābheda or oneness and difference is *logically contradictory* in traditional binary logic. If you have a single contradiction in a logical system, then you can prove anything. Thereby, you cannot assert any truths, because their opposites are also true. Likewise, you cannot assert any falsity because they are also true. Essentially, inconceivability within a binary logical system is equivalent to absolutely no truth. It is certainly less acceptable than modern science, other personal religions, impersonalism, and voidism.

Quantity vs. Quality Thinking

To solve that problem, we have to make Vedānta *conceivable*. This is again impossible in a binary logical system, so we have to change the logical system that only permits the truth to be either X or not-X. Our logical system has to permit the truth of both X and not-X without a contradiction. This is possible only if X and not-X are defined mutually, such that if one of them doesn't exist, then the other doesn't either. Now, X and not-X are true in different *contexts* not *universally*. Logical truths now include contextual truths rather than just permitting universal truths. Once we do that, then every conventional idea based on binary logic—numbers, geometry, space and time, the separability of objects, the reduction of the whole into parts—also changes.

All these changes can be summarized quite simply as the move from *quantities* to *qualities*. Quantity thinking involves binary logic, and quality thinking involves non-binary logic. That non-binary logic then leads us to Bhedābheda, or simultaneous oneness and difference. It is inconceivable in a worldview of quantities and conceivable in a worldview of qualities. Most people at present describe the world in terms of quantities, but all of Vedic philosophy is formulated in terms of qualities. There are three qualities of nature called sattva, rajas, and tamas. The soul has three qualitative aspects called sat, chit, and ānanda. God has many qualities like knowledge, beauty, power, wealth, fame, and renunciation. Each form of God differs in some qualities, and liberated souls are also different in their qualities.

Quality thinking requires the simultaneous existence of opposites such as hot and cold, bitter and sweet, and light and heavy because they are always defined by mutual opposition. We cannot separate them as *independent* things. However, only one of these two opposites can be considered true in a given situation. Thus, for instance, some object is hot while another is cold, some object is either bitter or sweet, and some object is either light or heavy.

Then, there are things that are *neither* of these opposites. For example, the quality of taste is neither bitter nor sweet; the quality of touch is neither hot nor cold. Finally, there are things that neither of these opposites *and* either of the opposites. For example, the mind is neither bitter nor sweet, and yet, it can be either bitter or sweet. Then the intellect is neither bitter nor sweet, but it can be both bitter and sweet in the sense that it can think of the distinction and relation between these opposites. Such distinguishing is required in the process of saying that something is more squarish in comparison to something that is more circular. Circularity is now a contextual truth perceived by the intellect through the capacity to see a distinction, contrast, and comparison, which in turn requires us to see opposites simultaneously.

This simple process of going from either-or to neither to neither with either to neither with both constructs a *logical hierarchy*. That logical hierarchy is also a quality hierarchy because the quality of taste is "higher" than the qualities of bitter and sweet, the concept of mind is "higher" than the qualities of taste and touch, and the judgment that sees either-or, neither, and both is "higher" than the mind which perceives neither or either. This higher truth is also *more* true than the lower truth because the lower truth is always a part of the higher truth. Thus, either-or is a part of neither, neither is a part of neither with either, neither with either is a part of neither with both.

These logical states can be used to construct a hierarchy of reality in which the material world is dominantly either-or, the Brahman realm is neither of these opposites, the Vaikuṇṭha realm is neither with either, and the Goloka realm is neither with both. Since Brahman, Vaikuṇṭha, and Goloka are neither, therefore, they are beyond material existence. But only Brahman is devoid of qualities. Vaikuṇṭha (neither with either) and Goloka (neither with both) are not devoid of qualities. If we cannot understand neither and both, then we cannot understand transcendence. But neither and both are impossible in binary logic, quantity thinking, and the idea of all truths being equally true.

The understanding of qualities needs numerous non-binary logical principles: (a) X and not-X can exist simultaneously, (b) they are not simultaneously true in all contexts, (c) something can be neither X nor not-X, (d) something can be neither X nor not-X and yet, either X or not-X, (e) something can be neither X, nor not-X, and yet, both X and not-X. You can go on combining these to get all kinds of categories that seem logically contradictory in binary logic. Their logical contradictoriness simply means that we can never understand these qualities in binary thinking, using quantities, employing linearity, where all truths are equally true, rather than more or less true.

The Need for Qualities in Vedānta

All problems of Vedānta interpretations are tied to the use of quantitative *analogies*. For example, Advaita uses the analogy of drop and ocean; they say: There is just the ocean, and no drops; the drops are created by dividing the ocean into parts, creating many drops. Each drop is qualitatively identical to the other drops because they are just water. Hence, we can ignore the qualitative differences between them, and just count the number of drops.

The fact is that in personalist philosophy, each soul is qualitatively unique. So, they are not identical drops of water. Rather, each drop is mixed with different portions of salt, sugar, and lemon, giving them unique flavors. The distinction between two souls is qualitative rather than quantitative. That is, one soul is different from another soul precisely because it is a different quality. Thereby, the ability to count them is a *consequence* of qualities. Similarly, two material objects are distinct based on qualities. We are able to count them due to qualitative differences. If we take out qualities, then we cannot identify, distinguish, and sequence things, and hence we cannot count them. Thereby, numbers or quantities are not the fundamental reality; the fundamental reality is the qualities that make things distinct, enabling counting.

Similarly, Viśiṣṭādvaita says that the soul and matter are properties of an object—God. But when the soul takes on a body, then one property (matter) becomes the property of another property (the soul). If we think in terms of quantities, then we can never understand this. For instance, if height and weight are two properties of a table, then height can never be *heavy* nor can weight be *tall*. But if you think in terms of qualitative properties, then color can be sweet and shape can be angry. Viśiṣṭādvaita is problematic under quantity thinking, as one property cannot be the property of another property. Then, we have to say that soul is an object and not a property.

That objectivity of the soul requires separation between the soul from God, which is called Dvaita. But it creates another problem—how can one object be created from a source object, without reducing the source? This is the issue of how can God remain complete after creation? You try to solve that problem without reducing God, and you will get an *ex-nihilo* doctrine.

Even in Bhedābheda, which uses whole-part analogies, whole and part are quantitative—the soul is a part of God like a finger is part of our body. It means if the soul is suffering, then God must be suffering, which transforms the soul's pain into God's pain, the soul's ignorance into God's ignorance, etc.

Contrast these with quality thinking. Now, the chair is furniture, but furniture is not the chair. A dog is an animal, but an animal is not a dog. Yellow is a color, but the color is not yellow. By using qualities, you start getting all the properties of Bhedābheda: Color and yellow are one because yellow is color; however, color and yellow are different because the color is not yellow.

Is this inconceivable? In binary logic, yes, because X is Y but Y is not X. But is it inconceivable in the sense that nobody can understand it? No, because everyone can understand that a dog is a mammal, but a mammal is not a dog. The quality system involves a conceptual *hierarchy*, like an inverted tree, while a quantity system involves object *linearity*—e.g., like points on a line.

Hierarchies are the norm in Vedic philosophy. In Sāñkhya for example, there is a hierarchy of material elements—from mahattattva to ahaṃkāra to buddhi to manas to indriya to tanmātra to bhūta. Vedic cosmology is about a hierarchy from higher planets to lower planets. And this hierarchy is constructed from three modes of material nature in which sattva is higher than rajas, which is higher than tamas. If we understand these qualities deeply, then rajas and tamas are mutually defined opposites, sattva is neither of these opposites, and śuddha-sattva is all of the three modes of nature in combination.

Thus, there is natural equivalence between (a) non-binary thinking, (b) hierarchies, (c) quality-based thinking, (d) oneness and difference, and (e) inconceivability of oneness and difference in quantity thinking, involving linearity, and binary logic, which is based on the separation of all things.

This is the essence of my *innovation* in Vedānta interpretation—change all analogies from quantities to qualities. Is it my *invention*? No, because quality thinking is pervasive in Vedic philosophy. Since there is innovation, therefore, there is a novelty. But because this is not an invention, therefore, there is continuity and greater consistency with the Vedic system as a whole.

Consistency vs. Completeness

The consequence of a qualitative reality is that *all* quantitative descriptions become *incomplete*. Why? Because you can say that X is Y, but you cannot say that Y is not X, as that will lead to a logical contradiction. Hence, you can only make *half* the claims. That is *incompleteness*. It was demonstrated in mathematics by Gödel's Incompleteness theorem, which says: "No system of arithmetic is both consistent and complete". What is arithmetic? It is quantity thinking. What is inconsistency? It is the inability to make all statements without contradiction. What is incompleteness? It is the ability to only make half the statements to avoid contradictions with the other half.

Now, we can show that all of modern science is incomplete due to quantity thinking. If it tried to be more complete, then it would become self-contradictory. By the same principle, we can say that since Vedānta systems have used quantitative analogies, therefore, they can only permit half the statements in the various Vedic texts, because the introduction of the other half would create inconsistency. Now, you can choose some subset of claims, and whichever subset is chosen, you will always get an incomplete doctrine. If you try to complete it, then your analogies will break down, and you will end up with numerous contradictions. The conclusion is that all scientific theories and all Vedānta doctrines are *incomplete* because of quantity analogies.

We can demonstrate this problem in numerous contexts individually, and I have done that over the last decade through my books. Every subject—mathematics, physics, biology, economics, computing—is either incomplete or inconsistent. Incomplete because it cannot answer all the questions of that subject. Any attempt to answer more questions leads to contradictions.

The same pattern of incompleteness vs. inconsistency also arises in the case of Vedānta doctrines. Advaita is most consistent, but also the most incomplete. As the doctrines evolved, they became more complete but more contradictions were introduced. Finally, over successive iterations of trying to become more complete, we arrived at Achintya Bhedābheda in which everything is contradictory. Now, we can say, as many Acharyas have said, that this is the most *complete* system of Vedānta. That is not false. However, we can also say that it is the most *inconsistent* system of Vedānta thus far.

When we say that it is most inconsistent, we are not contradicting the claim that it is the most complete system, and hence the most perfect in the sense of incorporating all Vedic statements. We are merely pointing out the inconsistency. Likewise, we don't stop at the criticism. We also trace this inconsistency to the use of quantity thinking and show how the solution to this inconsistency requires qualities, hierarchies, and non-binary logic.

The Necessity of Other Five Systems

The system of qualities, hierarchies, and non-binary logic is also Vedic philosophy, although it comes from the other five systems of philosophy—Sāñkhya, Yoga, Nyāya, Vaiśeṣika, and Mīmāṃsā. If we disregard these other five systems, and just employ ordinary intuitions about quantities to understand Vedānta, then we get either contradictions or incompleteness. Those contradictions in Vedānta come at the additional cost of contradictions with the other five systems because the other systems are talking about qualities, hierarchies, and non-binary logic, and we are interpreting Vedānta using quantities, linearity, and binary logic. Thus, we get contradictions *within* Vedānta and contradictions *with* the other five systems of philosophy. Conversely, if we take the six systems together, then we get completeness without contradictions. Therefore, we can interpret Vedānta itself using a system of qualities, hierarchies, and non-binary logic, but then we must also establish these using the other five systems. When we do both, then we solve all contradictions within a philosophy and between philosophies.

This is the genesis of the broader project entitled the Six Systems of Philosophy. It includes goals such as the (a) *unity* of Vedic philosophy, (b) making each system internally free of contradictions, (c) establishing Bhedābheda on a solid logical, scientific, and philosophical foundation, and (d) using that doctrine of Bhedābheda to attack the incompleteness of all quantity thinking, including science. All these goals either stand together, or they fall apart simultaneously; we cannot do just one of these.

Quantity thinking was introduced into Vedānta by Shankaracharya. We don't have to go into details, because even a superficial analysis will suffice: The whole is Brahman, and the parts are the souls and bodies. This whole, however, is *quantitatively big*. It is called *all-pervading*. It is also equated to space, which is quantitatively *infinite*. Some people have tried to equate this idea of Brahman to a quantum field. Why? Because that field is as big as the universe. When Brahman becomes quantitatively big, then it is no longer a person. Thereby, things don't originate from the personality of Godhead, because a person is quantitatively *finite*. All arguments of impersonalism against personalism are therefore based on quantity thinking.

It seems perfectly logical because (a) people are accustomed to quantity thinking, (b) it doesn't involve non-binary logic, (c) it is far simpler because you can forego conceptual hierarchies. In quantity thinking, there is no meaning in the world. Thereby, you can say that all rituals, yoga practices, deities of the Lord, and sanctified food, are meaningless things.

To support quantity thinking, Shankaracharya rejected the other five systems of philosophy based on non-binary logic, a system of qualities, and a hierarchical organization of these qualities. For example, the doctrine of Satkāryavāda in Sāñkhya says that the effect comes out of the cause because it is talking about how one quality is manifest from another quality. In quantitative thinking, nothing comes out of anything else. If we employ qualitative thinking, then māyā must also be produced out of Brahman, because it is one of the qualities of Brahman. This creates problems for Advaita, which wants to keep māyā separate from Brahman. To support his view, Shankaracharya rejected Satkāryavāda and thereby Sāñkhya. Similarly, Arthavāda in Mīmāṃsā says that the world is meaningful; examples include the use of mantras, rituals, deity worship, yoga practices, etc. which are meaningful activities. But Advaita has to insist that the world is completely meaningless, so it also rejected Arthavāda and Mīmāṃsā. Likewise, Vaiśeṣika says that individuals and qualities are eternally real, but Advaita says that individuality and qualities are illusions. Hence it rejects Vaiśeṣika. Then, Nyāya says that the parts exist in the whole eternally, and are manifest from the whole, but that is a problem for Advaita, which wants to describe the whole without parts. Therefore, Advaita rejects Nyāya. Finally, Yoga says that the soul as one of the parts of the whole (the Supreme Lord) must be devoted to the purposes of the whole and work according to His will. However, that is problematic for the oneness of Advaita, hence Advaita rejects Yoga as well.

Basically, the false doctrine of Advaita—rooted in quantity thinking—requires us to reject the other five systems of philosophy, and Shankaracharya used Vedānta Sūtra to derive the rejections of the other five systems. Overtly, he was saying: Vedānta is the conclusion of Veda, and other philosophies are not very important. But under the hood, he was taking out the foundation of qualities, non-binary logic, and hierarchies. That helped him reject devotion to the Lord, mantra chanting or deity worship, separate the material world from the Lord, assert that all individuality and qualities are illusions and that the whole is a partless entity while parts of the whole are illusions.

When Shankaracharya rejected all the five systems of philosophy, he took out the foundations of personalism in qualities, individuality, a common source of everything in the Supreme Lord, devotion to the Lord, and the logical process by which the whole divides into parts to create the manifest world. But it was made to appear as if Vedānta is supreme while the other systems of philosophy are secondary, irrelevant, unimportant. By creating a contradiction between Vedānta and the other five systems of philosophy, the claim was that qualities, individuality, devotion, forms of the Lord, mantras, deity worship, etc. are material, and they have to be rejected to embrace Brahman. The deeper claim was that there is no spiritual foundation for these things. Everyone knows that Advaita rejects the personality of God. What they don't know is that the philosophy of personalism rests upon hierarchies, qualities, and non-binary logic. You take out one, and you also lose the others.

How Paramparā Continuity Created Problems

When quantity thinking excludes many Vedic statements, impersonalism rationalizes the exclusion based on *logic*: If you introduce all these other Vedic ideas, then you will get contradictions. Thereby, Advaita stands supreme *because* it is the most consistent. Logic is now the tool to reject most Vedic statements. Of course, not everyone may accept logic as the supreme tool. So, they can bring other Vedic ideas into the fold to make Vedānta more complete, along with some additional contradictions. These contradictions invite many criticisms, and it becomes hard to defend the Vedānta system.

The problems of consistency vs. completeness in interpretations prevented successive Acharyas from accepting all Vedic statements or rejecting Advaita. They used Shankaracharya's commentary as the foundation, adding new claims that traded off completeness with consistency. Their argument was: Yes, there are many contradictions, but we assert that the Absolute Truth cannot be known by logic; It can only be known via devotion. Of course, you cannot say that our Vedānta system is totally illogical because that will make it vulnerable to even more attacks from Advaita. So, you play a careful juggling act of (a) not rejecting the basis of Advaita totally, (b) riddling yourself with many contradictions, and (c) not totally accepting all the Vedic statements.

The seeds of the dispute between jñāna and bhakti were sowed by this juggling act. The jñāni would say: You bhaktas are using logically contradictory arguments, based on *faith* in the Vedic scriptures. And the bhaktas would say: You the jñānis are relying on logic and reason to understand the Vedic scriptures. This dispute between jñāna and bhakti is almost synonymous with reason vs. faith in the West. However, its roots are quite different. We can see both the similarities and the differences between the two cases.

The result of this careful juggling act was the following: (a) the foundations of non-binary logics, quality thinking, and hierarchies, which are rooted in the other five systems of philosophy were rejected by all Acharyas as they continued using quantitative analogies, (b) they just added the individuality of the soul and God and devotional relationships, creating new contradictions.

In Brahma-Samhita 5.62, Śrila Bhaktisiddhānta Sarasvati criticizes all Vedānta interpretations prior to Achintya Bhedābheda in their historical order. He concludes: "These speculations have originated from Veda relying on the support of the Vedānta-Sūtra. In these speculations, although there is no truth that holds good in all positions, there is yet a certain measure of truth." This is a clear acknowledgment of the fact there are contradictory positions, which are not true in all cases; that is because X is Y but Y is not X. If we don't use non-binary logics, then X is Y is equated to Y is X, and you get a contradiction. If you say that X is Y, then you haven't said Y is not X, which is incomplete.

Śrila Bhaktisiddhānta Sarasvati then writes: "Not to speak of the anti-Vedic speculations Sāṅkhya, Patañjala, Nyāya, and Vaiśeṣika, nor even of Pūrva-mīmāṁsā which is fond of exclusive fruitive activity in conformity with the teaching of one portion of the Veda, the bodies of opinions detailed above have also come into existence by relying outwardly on the Vedānta itself. By discarding all these speculations, you and your bona fide community should adopt the ultimate principle identical with the doctrine of acintya-bhedābheda (inconceivable simultaneous distinction and nondifference). This will make you eligible for being a true devotee." This leads to questions.

For example, Sāñkhya is propounded by Lord Kapila in the Śrīmad Bhagavatam, and He is an incarnation of Lord Viṣṇu. So, how can Sāñkhya be considered anti-Vedic? Similarly, the aśtānga-yoga system is discussed by Lord Krishna in the Bhagavad-Gita. How can that be called an anti-Vedic system?

The answer is that the other five systems of philosophy have been rejected by all Acharyas because they were trying to maintain continuity with Shankaracharya in order to avoid too much criticism from the impersonalists. By limiting the number of changes made in a commentary, you reduce the criticism from the opponent, as they focus only on the few additional changes that you have made. Now, if you accept the other five systems, then you have to explain them too, which then requires commentaries on the other five systems. The devotional proponent will now criticize you on grounds of materialism because many systems of philosophy overtly deal with the material world. Thereby, you double the criticisms: (a) impersonalists will criticize anyway, and (b) even the personalists will abandon you because you are now entertaining "materialism" via the other five systems of philosophy.

Hence, even as later Acharyas changed a Sampradāya's view of the nature of soul and God, they did very little to the Advaita view of the material world. Thereby a big schism between Vedānta philosophy and the practice of the various Sampradāyas was created. For example, if you reject Mīmāṃsā, then it is very hard to justify mantra chanting or deity worship. If you reject Sāñkhya, then it is very hard to explain why some form of God is superior to another form due to a hierarchy of qualities. Then, if you reject Vaiśeṣika, you acknowledge that qualities are not real or eternal, although in practice you continue cooking various types of foods for the deity. Basically, the limitations of the philosophy create contradictions between theory and practice.

Fragmentation of the Vedic System

The Advaita system is not consistent with Purānas, Tantras, Pāñcharātra, or the four Vedas. Advaita was never trying to be consistent. It was merely trying to be consistent only with *some* Upanishads. Similarly, the Advaita system rejects the five systems of philosophy. The net result is a lot of fragmentation in the Vedic system. Those who want to follow Tantra split. Then, those who want to follow Puranas split. Then, those who like the Pāñcharātra system split. Then, those who want to preserve the four Vedas split.

Then, those who like the other five systems of philosophy split into different groups. Since these texts are also divided into Shaiva, Shakta, and Vaishnava texts, they split even further. For instance, Vaishnavism is split into Viśiṣṭādvaita, Dvaita, Śuddhādvaita, Bhedābheda, and Achintya Bhedābheda. For those who know the details, each of these has been further splitting into even more sects. For example, there are many subsects within the Gaudīya tradition that don't see eye-to-eye. Now, each group starts their own system of textual interpretations creating their own commentaries and paramparā system of religion.

The result is that nobody knows what the Vedic system really means. People equate "Hinduism" with so many philosophies that it is impossible for Hindus to even define their religion. Over time, they just replace religion with a culture or a "way of life". All these problems entail the gradual disintegration, deterioration, and eventual death of Vedic culture and philosophy.

Everyone in these fragmented systems can cite their authorities—their gurus. They can also cite some śāstra that they are based on. And yet, due to their inconsistencies, they stay away from the other systems. To the narrow-minded person, who looks within a particular Sampradāya, there can be strong arguments for maintaining continuity with their chosen system of gurus and texts. But in the broader sense, for someone looking at the entire Vedic system from the outside, there are so many conflicting Sampradāya.

This raises the question: What is śāstra? Is it just the books that I prefer to read? Or is it all the books in the Vedic system? Likewise, what is a guru? Is it just the particular system of gurus into which I have been initiated, or the other Sampradāya with different gurus, who assert different things, are also gurus? Whatever answer we give to such questions creates new issues. For instance, Lord Chaitanya took initiation from Madhava Sampradāya, but He did not take their Dvaita philosophy. He took Sannyasa initiation from the Advaita system, but He rejected their philosophy. He took the philosophy of Bhedābheda from Nimbārka Sampradāya along with Radha-Krishna worship, but not initiation from them. He accepted the worship of Lord Viṣṇu through salagram practiced in the Sri Sampradāya, but He did not emphasize it.

Reversing the Fragmentation

By hairsplitting these nuances, we are not getting closer to a conclusion. To fix these problems, we have to completely reject Shankaracharya's commentary and stop all attempts to maintain continuity. Instead, we have to bring back the system of qualities, hierarchies, and non-binary logic present in the five systems of philosophy and use that to reunify all the fragmentations.

This "clean-slate" approach may not be palatable to many people, but the alternative is much worse. When we reject Shankaracharya's commentary based on the principle that it uses quantity thinking and binary logic, we have to partially forego the successive commentaries that have tried to maintain continuity. However, that is not a *violation* of any paramparā, because it accepts all paramparā to be true in a certain sense. You don't contradict the tradition by calling table furniture. You contradict it by calling a table not a table. The bigger contradictions like oneness *and* difference are already there. When the goal is to make that contradiction conceivable, we are not deviating from the *conclusions*. The changes are in the interpretation of sūtras, which have to be explained. The benefit is that the Vedānta system will be consistent with the claims of all Vedic texts, all systems of philosophy, and all assertions can be accepted as true in a certain sense and in specific contexts.

The necessity of a clean-slate approach is that if we don't do such a thing, then we cannot present Vedic knowledge as a science, by the ordinary standards of being rational and empirical. We cannot apply the principles of Bhedābheda to interpreting the data of the ordinary world to show why separated thinking is false. And we can never arrest the rise of atheism, which relies on modern science, or impersonalism and voidism which try to simplify religion to a point where it loses all the subtleties and nuances of the Vedas.

An alternative interpretation of Vedānta is thus justified by: (a) unity among the Vedic traditions, (b) consistency with all Vedic texts, (c) consistency with the five systems of philosophy, (d) revival of qualities, hierarchies, and non-binary logic which make Bhedābheda conceivable, (e) the need of such conceivability to arrest the rise of materialism, atheism, impersonalism, and voidism, (f) make

Vedic philosophy relevant in today's world, and (g) lead an intellectual revolution quite like the European Enlightenment.

Any reasonable person can put all these benefits on one side, and contrast them with the benefits of sticking with a tradition or Sampradāya. I am convinced that an unbiased analysis will favor the clean-slate approach.

How

Philosophy of Text Interpretation

Everyone knows that words have many meanings. Some meanings are eliminated by taking the sequence of words in a sentence into account. For example, the word "President" can mean the "head of the state" or a particular person. "The President wants to meet you" requires us to treat the word "President" as a particular person. But "He was elected as President" requires us to treat "President" as the "head of the state". The problem doesn't end here. Certain whole sentences can have different meanings based on the sentences that were uttered *before* that sentence. This problem is easily demonstrable by using a single word sentence: "Yes". Are you going to the shopping mall? Yes. Are you going to sleep? Yes. The sentence "Yes" has a *possessed* meaning, but that is not enough. Its complete meaning is known only by the context in which it is used. This too may not eliminate all possible interpretations. To further fix the interpretations, we can apply additional constraints, namely, that the statements are not repeated or discontinuous. We can use also use other texts to constrain possible interpretations.

We have already noted the importance of other texts in understanding Vedānta. There is the constrain that we have to use qualities, hierarchies, and non-binary logic. We have noted the importance of maintaining consistency between Veda and Vedānta. Then, there are simpler constraints such as abiding by Sanskrit grammar and vocabulary. Finally, there is a constrain of contextuality based upon the strict sequencing of statements in a text, to ensure that they are interpreted (a) continuously, and (b) uniquely.

We can call these three constraints semantics, syntax, and logical progression. The last one is called nyāya-prasthān, which fixes the context and thereby restricts the possible interpretations of a sentence or word. The other two criteria of syntax and semantics still apply; nyāya-prasthān is an addition.

The Vedānta Sūtra is called nyāya-prasthān, and it is like a mathematical *proof*. You never repeat an assertion in a proof. Every statement means something new. This is *uniqueness*. Then, you cannot jump from one step in the proof to something that doesn't truly follow from the previous step. This is *continuity*. Continuity and uniqueness further constrain the possible interpretations of a text. That means that we are not permitting ourselves the freedom of interpretations based just on syntax and semantics.

Contextuality is evident in many places in Vedānta Sūtra. For example, the Sūtra "smṛrateśca" which means "also smriti" occurs many times. Talk about the qualification of a guru based on śrutī, and then say "also smriti". Talk about the nature of the Absolute Truth based on śrutī, and then say "also smriti". So, the sentence "also smriti" has no meaning independent of the context. Its meaning is always context-dependent. The question is: Why use context-dependent translation *sometimes*, and not at other times? And the answer is that contextuality must be used always. The result is logical proof in which nothing can be repeated and nothing can be missed.

Serialization Constraints Interpretations

While authoring this commentary I saw the practical use of this technique. There were occasions where I did not read the sūtra correctly and mistranslated it. Then I mistranslated the next sūtra, and the next one, and so on. On some occasions, I successfully mistranslated up to 20 sūtras, as there are many translations and possible interpretations of each sūtra.

Then I hit a brick wall, in the sense that, based on the previous succession of translations, I could never translate one of the later sūtras, because that sūtra can be understood only when the previous sūtras have been understood in a specific manner. The new sūtra translation did not make sense given the previous translations. I then retraced the journey backward and found the sūtra that I had misunderstood and restarted the process—sometimes redoing 20 sūtras all over again. The simple test was this: I should translate all the sūtras without discontinuity or repetition. Since there are 555 sūtras, there was always the risk that I could have reached the end of the book, hit a brick wall, and then had to start from the beginning again. I was prepared for that risk, to eliminate potentially erroneous translations of some of the sūtras.

By using this method, there were 3 occasions in which I found missing sūtras in the particular version of the Sanskrit text that I was relying on. The problem was that I simply wasn't able to translate *continuously* if a sūtra was missing; it created a discontinuity which made the interpretation of the subsequent sūtra impossible. I then looked at other versions of the text and found that that they had additional sūtras, which, when added, made the interpretation trivially easy. I could have skipped those sūtras and continued my translation if I was giving myself the liberty of free interpretations. I wasn't. The basic principle of logical progression of the proof caught missing steps in the proof.

The question is: Why are the sūtras in a specific order? Could we not rearrange them in another order? The answer is that if we rearrange them differently, then it would entail completely different interpretations. This is the problem of contextualization; any change in order drastically changes the meaning. This problem rarely arises in translating Upaniśads and Purānas, which is why it is possible to quote freely from these texts because a precise ordering of verses is not necessary. People accustomed to Purānas or Upaniśads may not understand this issue, because they are used to freely citing verses from different parts of the text, as the text is mostly context-independent.

The problem gets worse when some texts (e.g., Sāñkhya) bundle sūtras into *topics*. If we ignore the topic title, we cannot translate even the first sūtra under the topic, because the topic states what is being discussed, and the first sūtra makes the first statement within that topic, without mentioning the topic. For instance, the topic can be "The Discussion of Satkāryavāda", and none of the sūtras will use the word Satkāryavāda again because it is understood what we are talking about. The topic also constrains possible interpretations of the sūtras. We cannot deviate away from the topic. And yet, we must establish continuity, such that the last sūtra leads to the next topic.

One of the key differences between Purānas and Vedānta Sūtras is the use of pūrva-pakśa or an "objection" which is always inserted between two sūtras while doing a commentary although that objection is not present in the Vedānta Sūtras itself. I have used the format of questions instead of objections, but the two methods are equivalent. That question or objection sets the context of how the next sūtra has to be interpreted. If we change the questions, then we can change the interpretation of the next sūtra, but as I have noted above, we will hit a brick wall at some point where (a) the question or objection is being repeated, or (b) the question and answer do not make any sense given the previous sequence. Because an interpreter is "free" to insert an objection, there is seeming freedom in interpreting, but that freedom is permitted only if the entire sequence is unique and continuous.

How Uniqueness Improves the Commentary

When translations repeat their claims, then the redundancy of claims necessarily comes at the price of some missing conclusions. For instance, if you are allotted 5 sentences, and you repeat the same thing three times, then the total unique statements will be 3 instead of 5. This is very convenient if someone doesn't want to include all the conclusions of Veda in Vedānta. By repeating, you can ignore some essential conclusions. Conversely, by uniqueness, we can extract more essential conclusions from the same text.

One such conclusion is that Brahman has a masculine and feminine aspect, which are referred to as "two forms" or "two deities" a few times. We can scan all Vedānta commentaries, and not one describes them as the masculine and feminine form of Brahman. Thereby, the fact that we worship Sita-Rāma, Rādha-Krishna, Lakshmi-Nārāyana is *missing* from *all* Vedānta commentaries.

This is not a minor oversight either because it lies at the heart of all Vaishnava philosophy, and yet, it is missing even in Vaishnava commentaries. It arises because Vaishnava commentators were tweaking Shankaracharya's commentary, rather than redoing the entire sequence of sūtras. In Advaita, there is no need for masculine and feminine forms because Brahman is said to be genderless. But when it is missing even in Vaishnava commentaries, a deep schism between Vaishnava theory and practice is created.

How Continuity Improves the Commentary

Another issue we see in Vedānta commentaries is discontinuity. For instance, out of the blue, the commentary will state, "now we consider the objection from Buddhism" disregarding the fact that these texts predate Buddhism by centuries, so there cannot be any objection from Buddhism. Why does that arise? Because Shankaracharya was trying to respond to Buddhism.

The real questions are linguistic, such as "Can we speak of the Absolute Truth using language? Or is language a human creation that cannot be applied to the Absolute Truth?". These issues are not Buddhism but a form of impersonalism, also used by Buddhism. Therefore, we have to respond to that question, and in the process, we reject both Buddhism and impersonalism by recognizing the reality of language (which is called śabda-brahman) and its applicability to the Absolute Truth. However, if we narrow the scope to Buddhism, then we create a misunderstanding about what the sūtra truly means, permitting impersonal ideas such as "language is a human creation".

Who

The Problem of Arrogance

The above reasons for a new commentary are discussed in the introduction to my commentary, some detailed and some summarized. Anyone who reads the commentary can see them. And yet, I have received accusations of arrogance—i.e., that I consider myself more qualified than the previous Acharyas to think of commenting. Such accusations do not prescribe the qualifications of the person whose commentary would be acceptable. If we note that the Gaudīya tradition already has a commentary by Baladeva Vidyābhushan, then anyone who writes a commentary would be too audacious. That rules out the prospect of ever fulfilling Prabhupāda's instructions on Vedānta.

These accusations are a double-edged sword, because if I say that I'm qualified, then I am arrogant. But if I say that I'm not qualified, then I should not write. In both cases, the commentary must be rejected. In the former case, because I'm arrogant to consider myself qualified, and in the latter, because I'm humble to consider myself unqualified. But if we apply that yardstick to other commentaries, then the conclusion would be: Either they were too arrogant to write a commentary or their humility should have prevented them from authoring a commentary. We cannot decide anything like this. The argument of arrogance can never be answered satisfactorily by anyone.

While I was authoring this commentary, I used to tell my friend Ciprian that I can never finish it. I must have talked about my inadequacy to him almost a dozen times. Every step I moved forward did not increase my confidence in my ability. It always made me feel that I was not going to be able to complete it. I was constantly plagued by self-doubt and feelings of incompetence. When I finished the commentary, I did not feel a sense of achievement. I felt a sense of relief that it is over. Like a weight has been lifted off my shoulders.

So, if anyone thinks that this work is done out of a sense of pride in my ability, they are patently wrong. On the contrary, it was done out of a sense of duty, with constant doubts in my ability to fulfill the duty. I have constantly begged for Krishna's help, and I have constantly received guidance in the heart. But who is going to believe all these things? Perhaps nobody. They might accuse me of arrogance, because they don't know me, don't have all the facts, and because listening to such painful things is probably my destiny.

False Triumphalism

The root cause of such personal attacks is false triumphalism in the current state of understanding of Vedic philosophy. The uncurious mind is satisfied by a little knowledge because it cannot ask more profound questions. If the curiosities are satisfied, and no more questions are arising, then the uncurious mind considers additional books a nuisance: Why are these books required? They are certainly not required to satisfy my curiosities.

The most intelligent people can entertain alternative ideas temporarily, without getting disturbed by them. They know the arguments on both sides, and they know which argument is correct and why. But those who don't know the arguments on both sides, and why one argument is correct, can get disturbed by alternative viewpoints. Intelligent people strengthen their convictions through arguments. The less intelligent people are afraid that the alternative viewpoints or arguments will weaken their convictions.

Therefore, Vedic knowledge was formerly confined to the most intelligent people. The less intelligent people don't need to know everything. Keep them away from books, as they will get disturbed. Tell them a few basic things, which they can follow easily so that they are not overwhelmed. The difference was simply that those who did not read many books knew that others read them. They acknowledged their own ignorance and shortcomings and accepted that others were superior to them. When an issue arose, they approached those who knew more and requested clear answers.

But in this age, everyone thinks they know everything, although they cannot solve any open question or problem in any area of human inquiry. There are hundreds of big open issues in numerous areas of modern academia, which can be addressed through Vedic philosophy. But even those who claim to know Vedic philosophy are not able to use their professed knowledge to solve these problems. This is an indication that they do not know the philosophy, but they will not accept their ignorance. Such people, if called upon to address open questions, will say: All these are materialistic problems; we have already transcended into spirituality. They designate anyone who tries to answer these open questions as a "speculator" because they cannot see how such conclusions are entailed by Vedic philosophy. By name-calling, oversimplification, professing their own transcendence, and reducing everything to their level, such people drag everyone down. When standards are lowered in this way, then nobody can answer difficult questions or provide nuanced answers. Then, such people say: Nobody really knows.

We can see endless debates on forums that do not move the conversation forward. When the situation reaches a crisis, someone intervenes, makes a decision by popular vote or randomly, which is not convincing, but everyone watches helplessly and is forced to accept it. Despite the degrading quality of conversations, people are not able to accept that they don't know.

Of course, they accuse others of audacity, which is fine, because others are also accusing them of audacity. You add up all the audacious claims, and they amount to nothing. So, we don't need to give them any weight, because they are based on false triumphalism about knowing without knowing.

The Problem of Religious Finality

The problems of personal attacks on people trying to advance religion are also rooted in the desire for *finality*. People coming to religion want *finality*. Worldly knowledge is not final, because things keep changing. Religion gives people a sense of finality because scriptures do not change. But this finality is lost if scriptures are given new interpretations. That upsets people as they came to religion with the idea that religion gives the final truth.

Limiting the number of books, viewpoints, interpretations, eliminates that confusion and uncertainty. Religious finality demands that we should have read all the books, so the number of books cannot increase. By drawing an arbitrary limitation on what constitutes a religious text, they create a false sense of finality in religion—I have perfect truth, and it will never change.

However, we have to realize that God is infinite. The soul is eternal, and it spends eternity in trying to know that infinite. Finality has no room in religion because the soul can never know fully, and yet, there is an eternal endeavor to know more. That is not the same as constant changes in the understanding of the nature of the Absolute Truth. The difference is that improving religious understanding is always marked by *deepening* and *broadening*. Broadening means that more topics are now part of religion. And deepening means that we can understand a greater number of things using the same principle.

For example, Bhedābheda is generally understood to be a principle regarding the relation between soul and God—the two are neither identical nor completely different. But we can apply Bhedābheda even to quantum mechanics—two quantum particles are neither completely identical nor completely different. We can apply the same idea to sociology—individuals in society are not totally separate nor totally identical. Then, we can apply this viewpoint to psychology—the mind and body are not totally identical and not totally separate. This is what I mean by broadening and deepening. We can use Bhedābheda to understand the psyche, society, and quantum particles; this is the broadening of Bhedābheda. And yet, as we apply this philosophy, we begin to appreciate Bhedābheda in ever new ways. We are not talking about changing Bhedābheda to something unprecedented. We are talking about making Bhedābheda conceivable so that we can make it pervasive and use it in all subjects—psyche, society, and quantum particles.

This is not an attack on religious finality. But it is also not religious finality that rules out curiosity, expansion, advancement, and improvement of our understanding through applications of an idea. The books that apply Bhedābheda in different contexts are also not material books, even if they deal with the psyche, society, or quantum particles. They may not seem as much religious to a person who has a limited definition of religion confined to *one* application of oneness and difference that separates the material world from God. Those who see that integration, will not make such distinctions. Thereby, if we limit the number of books, to give ourselves a false sense of finality in knowledge, then we are exposing our disinterest in the infinite, a concomitant lack of curiosity, and pretentiousness of truly knowing.

At the least, Vedic religion is defined by *hunger*. Hunger for more. We satisfy *our* hunger by writing and reading books. But those who might not be hungry, find this problematic because they seek *finality*. Finality means no more books, and hunger means more books. To attain finality, one can reject all new books. And that is achieved by questioning an author's audacity to write.

There is no answer to such questions because they are produced by a desire for finality, discomfort with advancement, fear of losing one's conviction by entertaining alternative viewpoints, and a lack of curiosity. We cannot fix these issues, because the issues are in the reader and not in the author.

Ignoring Serious Everyday Issues

Philosophical debates have been ongoing since time immemorial, and we cannot stop them. That is because the human mind seeks perfection. The mind's desire for intellectual perfection is rooted in the soul's desire for perfection, knowing the Absolute Truth, and understanding our place in relation to that Absolute Truth. Philosophical debates also appear in the everyday world as debates about our place in the world. The real problem is that these philosophical debates have been mostly inconclusive.

For example, Greeks invented democracy because they realized that rational argument isn't taking anyone closer to the truth, because opposite positions are true in different contexts, although not universally true. Greeks believed that truth must be universal, not contextual. Socrates, considered the greatest of Greek philosophers, spent a lifetime in such arguments only to realize at the time of death that he had not reached any conclusion. Therefore, some people might say: What is the use of all these debates? After all, they are never conclusive and final. But that is not going to put philosophical debates to an end, because of the mind's and soul's desire for perfection.

We must understand the real causes of inconclusivity in debates. Why are arguments and philosophical views inconclusive? As we have discussed, the root problem is that any conversation that employs binary logic, quantities, and linearity is going to be either contradictory or incomplete. That means, either you cannot know everything, or you believe in contradictory ideas.

Democracy or autocracy is not the answer to this problem. The answer is a better way of reasoning. Also, reasoning is not limited to theology. It applies to every single conversation and decision you make. There is a better method to reason, which is that we can make the simultaneous truth of X and not-X conceivable, such that X is true in one context and not-X is true in another context. That way, everyone can stop arguing endlessly, because they have a method for deciding what should be done in a specific situation.

The Absolute Truth is both sour and sweet. But if we don't taste the Absolute Truth, then it is neither sour nor sweet. When we taste the Absolute Truth, sometimes it is sour and sometimes it is sweet. But if we persist, then over time, we can see that it is both sour and sweet. The same applies to every relative truth; it can be either-or, neither, or both. For the last 2500 years, Western philosophy has pursued the either-or logic, and for the last 2500 years, voidism and impersonalism have pushed the neither logic. So, when we want to go to the both logic which doesn't contradict either-or and neither, then we need a serious overhaul in thinking, beginning with logic.

If we do not accept that overhaul, then all conclusions based on binary thinking will be no better than a coin toss. We might as well stop arguing because whatever we conclude, will be wrong 50% of the time. That means half of all our choices are wrong. Half of everything that we are doing is adharma. Half of everything we consider true is not true in a situation.

Those who accuse me of pride or arrogance are thinking "I don't need this". This is not true. They may not *want* it, but they *need* it. That is because everyone is stuck in wrong decisions by using binary logic, and its attendants. When something is needed by everyone, then supplying that need is not arrogance. It is actually a service to everyone. But if someone doesn't see that need and necessity, then they can call it arrogance because they are not thinking about their own good, how they are stuck in mindless inconclusive debates because they cannot decide what is true in a given situation.

Democracy is about serving one's own needs. Autocracy is about forcing one's needs on others. But there is something beyond these two—serving everyone's needs. When everyone's need is served without forcing them, then there should be no issue if serving them is also my need and want..

www.ingramcontent.com/pod-product-compliance
Lightning Source LLC
Chambersburg PA
CBHW022157160726
48282CB00024B/226